ESS... SU... G...

HOWARD BOOKS
A DIVISION OF SIMON & SCHUSTER
New York London Toronto Sydney

TO LIVING ON YOUR OWN

Money • Relationships • House & Car Hunting • Health Care
Insurance • Voting • Cleaning • and Much More

SHARON B. SIEPEL

Published by Howard Books, a division of Simon & Schuster, Inc.
1230 Avenue of the Americas, New York, NY 10020
www.howardpublishing.com

Library of Congress Cataloging-in-Publication Data

Siepel, Sharon B.
Essential survival guide to living on your own / Sharon Siepel.
p. cm.
1. Life skills. 2. Young adults—United States—Life skills guides.
3. Living alone—United States. I. Title.
HQ2037.S54 2008
646.7—dc22

2007033998

ISBN-13: 978-1-4165-4969-7
ISBN-10: 1-4165-4969-2

10 9 8 7 6 5 4 3 2 1

HOWARD and colophon are registered trademarks of Simon & Schuster, Inc.

Manufactured in the United States of America

For information regarding special discounts for bulk purchases, please contact:
Simon & Schuster Special Sales at 1-800-456-6798
or business@simonandschuster.com.

Edited by Between the Lines
Cover design by Rex Bohn
Interior design by Stephanie D. Walker
Illustrations by Rex Bohn

To Austin, Kyrie, Savannah, and Ethan
Act justly,
love mercy,
and walk humbly with your God
(Micah 6:8).
(Plus follow the advice in this book.)
Love, Mom

Contents

Acknowledgments

The day Howard Books contacted me regarding publishing this book, the U.S. Navy Reserves mobilized my husband. He left a month later to spend more than a year in Iraq, leaving me with four kids and an incomplete manuscript. To say I owe a huge debt of gratitude to those who supported me would be a gross understatement.

Many thanks . . .

To God: for Your sense of timing, sense of humor, and unfailing love.

To Kevin: for your unwavering belief in me, your strength, and your willingness to sacrifice in order to serve others. You lead by example. I am proud to call you husband.

To my parents: for being my first editors and fans.

To my in-laws: for being there, cheerleading, and child care.

To my kids: for allowing me to write and "not work for you" for a season.

To my siblings: for early morning phone calls, frequent e-mails, and your prayers.

To Barbara and Liisa: for hanging in and hanging out with me.

To the staff at Faith Church: for your incredible enthusiasm, grace, and dinner every Tuesday for a year! I am blessed to serve alongside you.

To Faith Writers: for your encouragement, critique, and companionship on this journey.

To my Faith Church family: for your prayers, kind deeds, and many meals.

To Write to Publish: for giving me knowledge and opportunity.

To Denny, Chrys, and the rest of the Howard Books family: for caring about my book and my family.

To Dawn at Between the Lines: for adding clarity to my vision for this project.

INTRODUCTION
ON YOUR OWN

You've packed up all your belongings: clothes, bedding, your music, perhaps a computer and a few family photos. Now you are moving out of your parents' house and into your own place—maybe an apartment or a dorm room or house. You're ready. So ready. At least you think so. You certainly want to be. That's where this book comes in. This guide was created to equip you not merely for surviving on your own but for thriving—successfully entering and navigating the world of adulthood. With God's grace, you can do just that.

Essential Survival Guide touches on almost every aspect of day-to-day life. Whether you're doing your first load of laundry, balancing your checkbook, or selecting a church, this book offers guidance and suggestions for you to consider in your decision-making process. Let the adventure begin!

PART 1

GETTING THROUGH THE DAY

Being on your own is all about making decisions. Big decisions: What do I want to do with my life? And lots of little decisions: What kind of laundry detergent should I buy? What should I have for breakfast? To start, let's go up to 30,000 feet and look at the big decisions. Then we'll come back down and tackle the everyday nitty-gritty.

Chapter 1

Setting Goals and Priorities

So, who do you want to be when you grow up? Not *what* do you want to be, but *who* do you want to be? What kind of person do you want to become? What legacy do you want to leave behind? What is your passion? Your calling?

If you were stranded on a deserted island where money, time, people, and resources were not an issue and you were told to choose one thing—one task—to do, what would that be?

Let me give you a little hint: it's not all about the money. When I ask young adults what career they're going to choose, the most popular response is "I don't know. I just want to make lots of money."

Do a job for fifteen years just for the money and your life will be the equivalent of eating cold, stale french fries every morning. Dreary. Do something you're passionate about or that you feel called to do, and then success, contentment—and perhaps money—are possible.

Don't have a clue? That's okay. That's what this time in your life is all about. Explore your options. Gain experiences. Read chapter 60 about volunteering and broadening your world of possibilities.

Okay, now down to 10,000 feet.

Goals are simply dreams written down on paper. They're destinations at which we wish to arrive. Goals don't have to be set in stone. Life happens, and things change. Goals just start us down a path and help us to look up from our feet to the horizon of the future.

You can start small, with goals for this month, and work your way up to the bigger stuff. Try listing some things you'd like to accomplish in various stages using the list below.

My goals

For the next thirty days: ______________________________

____

For the next three months: ____________________________

____

For the next six months: ______________________________

____

Resources to help discern your gifts, passions, career options

- *What You Do Best in the Body of Christ* by Bruce L. Bugbee
- *S.H.A.P.E.: Finding and Fulfilling Your Unique Purpose for Life* by Erik Rees
- Myers-Briggs Type Indicator (www.myersbriggs.org)
- *48 Days to the Work You Love* by Dan Miller (www.48days.com)

For the next year: ____

____

For five years from now: ____________________________________

____

For ten years from now: _____________________________________

____

What I need to do to reach my goals

1. ____
2. ____
3. ____
4. ____
5. ____

Things I need to avoid in order to reach my goals

1. ____
2. ____
3. ____
4. ____
5. ____

Priorities

Now that you've set some goals for yourself, it's time to set priorities. Your priorities will determine how you spend your time, your resources, and your gifts—in other words, how you live your life as you try to achieve your goals.

Rank the following items, 1 being the most important thing to you, 11 being the least important.

___	God, spiritual life	___	Family
___	Spouse/boyfriend/ girlfriend	___	Money
___	Education	___	Work
___	Serving others	___	Physical health
___	Friends	___	Housework
___	Free time/entertainment		

All eleven items will more than likely be part of your life. The key is finding the proper balance. Priorities help us to find and keep that balance.

What was your first priority? ______________________________

Why? ______________________________

____

How are you going to keep that priority? ______________________________

____

What was number 11? ______________________________

Why? ______________________________

____

____

What do you need to do to keep your priorities in balance? ______________________________

____

____

____

Idea!

When life is busy, one way to balance your priorities is to combine them. Serve others with a group of friends. Work as an intern in the area of your college major and receive credit.

Chapter 2

Getting Organized

Get a planner. Write things down. Not just what you *have* to do, like papers, projects, etc., but things you *want* to do. Want to spend time with a friend? Write it down. Want to volunteer with Habitat for Humanity? Write it down.

Most opportunities in life won't come your way unless you plan for them to happen. I'm not talking about becoming a schedule slave; but looking at our weeks or months in the context of all that we have to do, all the places we have to be, and also our deepest desires that bring meaning to our lives. Being organized in this way helps maintain a balance between our immediate needs and long-term goals.

Let's say your priorities are (1) God, (2) education, (3) work, (4) friends, (5) serving others, (6) free time, and (7) household chores. Open your planner or calendar. Look at the next few weeks and write down when you plan to do the things that correspond to those priorities. You can use this example as a guide.

Sunday	Monday	Tuesday	Wednesday	Thursday	Friday	Saturday
Church	Class	Study	Class	Do laundry and study	Class	Work
Play bas-ketball with friends	Work	Class	Help with after-school program	Class	Work	Work or volun-teer
Free time	Study	Clean house	Class	Study at library with friends	Free time	Go to Bible study with friends

PART 2
MONEY, MONEY, MONEY

Want to eat? You need money.

Want to have clothes? Having money is a must.

Electricity, phone, car, gasoline—all cost money.

With money being such a huge factor in how we live, it's easy to become slaves to the almighty dollar. But the Bible says, "Keep your lives free from the love of money and be content with what you have, because God has said, 'Never will I leave you; never will I forsake you'" (Hebrews 13:5). This chapter offers beginning steps to becoming financially wise.

Chapter 3

Budgeting 101

Budgeting allows you to control your money rather than money controlling you. The goal of budgeting is to spend *less* money than you make and to decide in advance where your money is going.

Basic budget worksheet

Monthly income: ____________

Monthly expenses

Fixed expenses (expenses that stay the same every month)

Tithe/charitable giving ____________

Utilities ____________

Insurance ____________

Car loan ____________

Student loans ____________

Phone bill ____________

Internet service ____________

Other payments ____________

Total fixed expenses ____________

A. Monthly income __________ – Fixed expenses __________ = The amount you can spend on your variable expenses __________

Variable expenses (expenses the amounts of which can change from month to month)

Groceries ____

Household items (stamps, lightbulbs, plants, etc.)______________

Personal items (toiletries, dry cleaning, haircuts, etc.) _________

Transportation (gas, parking, bus pass, auto maintenance, etc.) ____

Clothing ____

Savings ____

Entertainment (cable, movies, eating out)____________________

Other____

Total variable expenses ____________________________________

B. Amount from Line A ____________ – Total variable expenses____________ = ____________

Budgeting resources

- Dave Ramsey, money management expert (www.daveramsey.com)
- Crown Financial Ministries (www.crown.org)

Take your total variable expenses and subtract them from total on line A. The answer must be greater than zero! If the answer is a negative number, reduce your budgeted numbers, starting with the variable expenses first.

WARNING—Do not adjust groceries and clothing to zero. You have to eat and have clothes on your back . . . you just don't have to eat sushi and wear designer clothing.

Chapter 4

A Word about Debt

Debt stops dreams.

A typical credit card purchase ends up costing 112 percent more than if you'd used cash. A $1,000 charge on an average credit card will take almost twenty-two years to pay and will cost more than $2,300 in interest if you make only minimum payments.[1] So that $1,000 purchase really costs you $3,300.

But what if instead of making the credit card companies rich, you invested in yourself? If you save $218 per month for twenty-five years, you would retire with $1,354,930.00!

How to use a credit card wisely

1. Try to pay off the balance every month.

2. Only use the credit card for:

   - business expenses for which you will be reimbursed. (Remember to pay the credit card charges when you receive reimbursement.)
   - renting a car. (Most car rental companies accept only major credit cards for payment.)
   - medical emergencies.
   - auto repairs that affect your ability to drive the car.
   - replacing broken major appliances if they are absolutely necessary (like water heater, stove, or refrigerator).

3. DO NOT use your credit card to purchase:

   - clothes.
   - food, whether at restaurants or the grocery store.
   - music.
   - books.
   - entertainment.
   - haircuts.
   - games—computer, video, or otherwise.

   Purchase these items with cash as you can afford them out of your income.

Chapter 5

Banking

Opening your first bank account as an adult is a big deal. Banks have restrictions on the access minors have to their money. But as soon as you turn eighteen, you're on your own. So here are some banking basics you need to know.

Types of financial institutions

- Commercial banks deal mainly with business and industry.
- Savings banks serve individuals.
- Savings-and-loan institutions concentrate on providing home mortgages.
- Credit unions were established to provide emergency loans, but they also offer checking and savings accounts as well as

many other banking services. However, membership may not be open to everyone.

At one time these various institutions provided separate services, but today they offer many of the same ones. So it's best to shop around for the financial firm that serves you best.

Types of accounts

Savings account: This is where you place the money you want to set aside so it can earn a higher interest rate. Normally, no fees are charged to withdraw funds, but this is not where you'll want to put the money you use in the course of everyday living.

Checking account: This is where you put the money you need to live off of every month. You can make withdrawals from this account via check, ATM, debit card, or electronic transfer. Usually little or no interest is earned on this account. Some banks charge fees for various aspects of this service. You will also have to pay for your own checks.

NOW (Negotiable Order of Withdrawal) account: This is a checking account that earns interest but also requires you to maintain a minimum balance.

Money market deposit account: This is a savings account, though it offers some services you'd find with a checking account. Funds kept in this kind of account earn interest at a higher rate than a typical savings account, but you may have more transaction restrictions.

Certificates of Deposit (CDs): Investment savings accounts that "lock in" your funds at a set interest rate for a fixed period of time, such as six months or a couple of years. Penalties are assessed for early withdrawal. This is where you would keep money that you want to save, not spend.

Questions to ask when comparing banks

- Is there a monthly fee for the account?
- Does the account earn interest? If so, how much?
- Is there a fee for ATM transactions?
- Is there a limit on how many withdrawals you can make per month?
- Does the account come with a debit card?
- Can you use your debit card as a credit card?
- Does the debit card earn you any rewards, like cash back or airline miles?
- Does the institution offer online banking? Is there a fee?
- Can you pay bills online? Does it cost anything to do that?

Chapter 6

Checking It Out

How to write a check

1. In the space provided, write the date, including month, day, and year.
2. Where it says "Pay to the order of" or "Payable to," write the name of the person or company to whom you are writing the check.
3. In the small square space with the dollar sign, write the numerical dollar amount of the check. (Example: $235.24)
4. On the next line, under the "Payable to" line, write the dollar amount using words for dollar amounts and fractions for cents. (Example: Two hundred thirty-five and 24/100)
5. Sign your name on the lower right line.

6. On your check register (the lined booklet that came with your checks), record the check number, date, payee, and dollar amount.
7. Subtract the check amount from your balance so you know how much money you have left.

How to endorse a check

In order to cash, deposit, or transfer a check from someone else, you must sign (endorse) the back of the check. Most checks have lines printed on the back to use for endorsing. Do not write below these lines.

A check can be endorsed in one of three ways:

- ***Blank endorsement:*** Sign your first and last name only on the back of the check. This allows anyone to deposit the check, cash it, or deposit a portion and get the rest in cash. Wait until you're at the bank to endorse the check. If someone else gets hold of your signed check, they can deposit or cash it.
- ***Restricted endorsement:*** Sign your full name on the back of check and write "For deposit only" and your account number under your signature. Now the check can only be deposited into your account. You cannot get cash back. When depositing checks through the mail or ATM, always write "For deposit only."
- ***Endorsing to another person:*** To sign your check over to someone else so that person can cash or deposit it, print on the back of the check, "Pay to the order of" on the top line. Under that, print the person's first and last name. Place your signature on the next line.

How to enter items in your checkbook

A checkbook or register comes with the checks that you order. Keep your checkbook with you so can enter any checks, purchases, withdrawals, or deposits when they take place. If you don't have your checkbook with you, make sure you keep all receipts and write down any check information. Update your checkbook at the end of every day.

The typical check register has a line that looks something like this across the top:

Number	Date	Code	Description of Transaction	Payment/Debit	Fee	Tax	Deposit/Credit	$

The lines below usually alternate between two colors, like white and gray. Use two lines per transaction and record information as described below.

- ***Number:*** Write the check number if you are using a check to make a purchase or payment.
- ***Date:*** Write the month and day (example: 5/4 for May 4).
- ***Code:*** Use this space to note the type of transaction you are making other than check writing. (Example: DC for debit card, D for deposit, AP for automatic payment, ATM for cash withdrawals at ATMs)
- ***Description of Transaction:*** Write the name of the business or person to whom you wrote the check or otherwise made payment. Below that, on the next line, record what the payment was for (e.g., Wal-Mart [on the first line], groceries [on the second line]). This will help you see where your

money is going, and the information will come in handy at tax time.

- ***Payment/Debit:*** Write the amount of the check or other withdrawal from your account.
- ***Fee:*** Record any banking or ATM fees.

Banking Tip

Avoid bank fees by using your debit card as a credit card instead of a debit card. The money will still come directly out of your checking account.

- ***Tax:*** Check if the item could be deducted from your taxes (such as a donation to a charity, nonreimbursed business expense, or medical expense).
- ***Deposit/Credit:*** Write the amount of any deposits or credits made to your account.
- ***$:*** On the very first $ box at the top of the page, write your account balance. When entering a transaction, write down amount of payment or credit on the top line of your entry. Put a minus sign (–) in front of a payment and a plus sign (+) in front of every credit. Do the math and add or subtract the amount from your balance. Enter the new balance on the second line of your entry.

Chapter 7

Keeping Things Balanced

It's important to keep a running balance of the funds in your checking account as well as balancing your checkbook against your bank statement every month. If you have a computer, the easiest way to do this is by purchasing software such as Quicken or Microsoft Money. These programs make it easy to electronically track your banking transactions as well as help you balance your checking account.

Balancing your checkbook in five easy steps

1. Write down the ending balance shown on your monthly bank statement.
2. List all deposits you've made that are not on the bank statement.

3. List all the check amounts and other withdrawals that you have made that are not included on the bank statement.
4. Add the total amount of the deposits in step 2 to the ending balance in step 1.
5. Subtract all of the withdrawals in step 3 from total in step 4. This total should match your checkbook balance

Checkbook balancing worksheet

Ending balance shown on bank statement ________

Add all deposits not shown on bank statement ________

Subtotal ________

Subtract all checks, withdrawals, and fees not shown on statement ___

Total adjusted ending balance ________

Current checkbook balance ________

Your checkbook is balanced when the total adjusted ending balance on your monthly bank statement equals the ending balance in your checkbook.

Running balance

Keeping a running balance means adding the money you put into your account and subtracting the money you take out on a daily basis. Money disappears quicker than you think. Knowing exactly what you have in your account will save you a lot of grief.

Bounce, bounce, bounce

Your check bounces when you don't have enough money in your account to cover the amount of the check. Bad things happen when this occurs. You will be charged fines by both your bank and the business to which you wrote the check. These fines could be as high as $75 per check bounced. Ouch. Writing a bad check, or writing a check knowing you don't have enough money in your account is a crime and can land you in jail. Don't do it!

Chapter 8

How You Rate

Everyone who has ever used a credit card, gotten a car loan, or signed a payment contract, like a cell phone agreement, has a credit record. A business or lending institution, before extending credit to you, will check your credit record to decide whether lending you money is a good risk. Having a good credit rating (also called a credit score) is important if you ever want to buy a car or a house.

Credit history is rated on a scale from 300 to 850, and the higher your score, the better. A score of 650 or higher is considered a good rating. Scores from 620 to 649 are considered satisfactory. With this score, you may have to provide extra documentation (such as a list of assets or your employment record) to prove that you are a good risk to a lender. Remember, a loan officer is going to lend money only to someone who shows he or she can pay back the amount borrowed. With a credit rating below 620 you will be charged much higher interest rates, if you are able to obtain a loan at all.

How to earn a high credit score

- Always make your payments on time.
- Don't open too many lines of credit.
- Limit the number of times you or a business inquires about your credit score. Multiple inquiries lower your score.
- Don't file for bankruptcy. Bankruptcy will significantly lower your credit rating for ten years.
- Check with credit bureaus to make sure all your information is correct.
- Close any lines of credit you're not using. Even after you pay off credit cards, the line of credit will remain open, affecting your credit score, until you request that the account be closed.

Credit report scams

You've heard companies advertise on TV, radio, and the Internet, offering to provide you with a "free credit report." Many of these companies use this ploy to get you to sign up for their fee-based service. They may even offer a "free 30-day trial." When you sign up for your "free" report, these companies ask for your credit card number. They're counting on your forgetting to cancel their services after the free trial period. At the end of the 30-day trial, they bill your credit card. To find out how to get a truly free credit report, see the next section.

How many is too many?

Credit bureaus look at how many lines of credit you have open, what you owe on those lines, and how much you can still borrow. For example, let's say you have a department-store credit card with a balance of $500, but your limit is set at $1,000. The credit bureaus take into account not only what you owe but also what more you can spend. In this case, they know it's possible for you to run up another $500 of debt. If your income does not allow for you to comfortably pay off $1,000, your credit score is lowered.

To prevent this scenario, limit your lines of credit to the absolute minimum. This may mean having only one, or none!

How to check your credit rating for free

As of September 1, 2005, everyone in the United States is entitled to get one free copy of his or her credit report annually from each of the three major credit bureaus. The **only** Web site authorized to provide you with a free credit report is www.annualcreditreport.com.

Alternatively, you can send a written request to each of the three major credit bureaus. Include your full name, address, Social Security number, and any addresses you've lived at in the last five years.

These are the three major credit bureaus:

- Equifax (www.equifax.com)
- Experian (www.experian.com)
- TransUnion (www.transunion.com)

Chapter 9

The Taxman

Check any of the following that are true.

- ☐ Someone else claimed you as a dependent on his or her income tax return, but you earned more than $5,150 this year.
- ☐ You are single, had a gross income of $8,450 or more, and are not anyone's dependent.
- ☐ You are married, filing jointly, and you have a combined gross income of $16,900.
- ☐ You are married, filing separately, and earned $3,300 (or more) this year.
- ☐ You are head of household and earned $10,850 or more.
- ☐ You are self-employed and earned $400 or more.

- ☐ You are a widow or widower with dependent children and earned $13,600 or more.

If you checked *any one* of these items, then guess what?

You have to file an income tax return! Giddy-up!

Annual income tax returns are due April 15, or the following business day if April 15 falls on a weekend or holiday. This means you must mail (not just drop in the box but actually have postmarked) or file your income taxes before midnight on the due date.

Tax forms and instructions are available by mid-January. You can pick up paper forms for free at some post offices and libraries, or download forms online at www.irs.gov.

Documents and records you need to keep for tax time

- Copies of all W-2 forms
- Copy of completed tax form from the previous year
- Receipts for charitable donations (gifts of money or material items to nonprofit organizations)
- Receipts for job-related expenses (like travel and meals)
- Child-care receipts
- Mortgage statements
- Medical bills
- Education expenses
- Moving expenses
- Uniform receipts

- Mileage for traveling to volunteer or military (National Guard or Reserves) jobs

Tax deductions

You can deduct some items and expenses from your taxes, but you have to keep paperwork documenting that the deductions are legitimate. To make filing taxes easier, create a folder marked "Taxes," and file all the financial records and receipts you receive throughout the year into it. Depending on your circumstances, you may or may not be allowed to deduct anything from your tax bill, but at least this way you'll have your records ready.

For more info visit the following Web sites:

- Internal Revenue Service (www.irs.gov)
- H&R Block (www.hrblock.com)
- Intuit, Inc. (http://turbotax.intuit.com)

Oh, gross!

Your gross income is all the money you made *before* your employer took out any taxes, other deductions, or allowances. All figures are based on your gross income.

Are you a dependent?

To be someone's dependent, you must . . .

- be that person's child, stepchild, foster child, sibling, or descendent
- reside more than six months a year with that person
- be under the age of nineteen, or if you are a full-time student, under the age of twenty-four
- not provide for more than half of your living expenses.

PART 3
GETTING YOUR OWN PLACE

Whether it's a dorm room, apartment, or house, getting your own place goes beyond having a place to sleep—it's establishing your own home.

Before getting a place, consider what you want to use your home for. Do you just need space for a bed, or do you need enough room to entertain family and friends?

Think about what you want your first home to be. Safe? Friendly? Clean? Convenient? Comfortable? Charming? Exciting? Affordable? Spacious? Practical? Extravagant?

Consider your housing priorities, then use this section to help you find the right place for you.

Chapter 10

Finding Home Sweet Home

A home might be sweet, but it sure isn't cheap. And they call it house "hunting" for a reason. This chapter includes a list of things you need to have in order to rent a place to live, plus some forms to make house/apartment hunting easier.

Money you may have to have before you rent

- Application deposit (refunded when you sign the lease)
- Credit report fee (see chapter 8)
- First month's rent
- Security deposit (usually equals one month's rent)
- Money for necessary items to set up house, such as trash cans, shower curtains, or window blinds

- If a broker is involved, a fee may be required
- Deposit for utilities (including electricity, heating fuel, telephone, and cable)
- Money to furnish and stock apartment with necessities for living

Other things you'll need

- Two references—two adults (not your buddies) who will vouch that you are a responsible, good person
- Checking account
- A steady source of income

Apartment or rental house evaluation forms

When you visit one apartment after the next, they tend to blur together, and it's easy to forget which one had what features. Download this online form at http://www.simonsays.com/content/book.cfm?tab=1&pid=614860&agid=38, make copies and take them with you to take notes. Your notes will come in handy when trying to remember what you liked and didn't like about each place.

Complex ______________________________

Address ______________________________

Phone ______________________________

Web site ______________________________

Distance from work/school ______________________________

Distance from church ______________________________

Distance from activities/social life ______________________________

Interior features:

How many square feet____________________

Space needed ______________ # of bedrooms: _______________

# of bathrooms: _______________ # of closets: _______________

Check all that apply:

- ☐ shower
- ☐ bathtub
- ☐ dishwasher
- ☐ laundry hookups
- ☐ good water pressure
- ☐ air conditioning
- ☐ heat
- ☐ refrigerator
- ☐ microwave
- ☐ window blinds
- ☐ adequate lighting
- ☐ good cell-phone reception
- ☐ cable
- ☐ Internet access
- ☐ handicap accessible
- ☐ additional storage
- ☐ pets allowed
- ☐ smoke detectors
- ☐ fire extinguishers
- ☐ locks on doors
- ☐ pest control
- ☐ well-maintained/clean

List other pros: ____

____

List any cons:____

____

Exterior features

Check all that apply:

- ☐ laundry facility
- ☐ mailbox
- ☐ parking lot
- ☐ garage

- ☐ security system/doorman
- ☐ safe neighborhood
- ☐ near grocery store
- ☐ fenced yard
- ☐ gym
- ☐ good schools
- ☐ manager lives on grounds
- ☐ well-lighted exterior
- ☐ near mass transit
- ☐ yard
- ☐ pool
- ☐ garbage removal/Dumpster
- ☐ well-maintained/clean

Is the apartment on the first floor? ______________________

What is the noise level? ______________________________

Notes: ______________________________________

____

____

____

____

Renting tips

- Rent should equal no more than 25 percent of your monthly income. If you earn $2,000/month, your rent should be $500 or less.
- Ask the neighbors about noise levels, whether they've had any maintenance issues regarding the apartment/house, and how safe they feel in the neighborhood.
- Visit on a weekend afternoon or weekday evening and observe people. Is this a community in which you can easily make connections?
- Call the local police department and ask about the crime rate in the neighborhood and if any convicted sex offenders live nearby.
- www.familywatchdog.us will also give you the names and addresses of convicted sex offenders.

Chapter 11

Before You Sign Anything

Before you sign a lease or rental agreement, check the contract for the following:

- What is the length of the lease?
- Under what conditions can the landlord or tenant (you) break the lease?
- Who is responsible for maintenance and repairs?
- Can your rent be raised?
- How many people are permitted to occupy the apartment/house?
- Are you permitted to sublease a room?
- Are pets allowed?
- What do you have to do to get your security deposit back?

- When is the rent due?
- What are the fees for paying the rent late?
- Who is responsible for paying the utilities?

Remember: Whoever signs the lease is the one obligated to pay the rent. If you have roommates, have them sign the lease with you, or have the landlord draw up individual leases for each occupant.

Get renter's insurance!

Say an electrical fire ignites in your living room. The flames destroy your couch, television, and stereo. Your landlord's property insurance covers the damage done to the building; it does not cover your belongings.

Having renter's insurance protects your personal property against fire, vandalism, and theft. Before moving into your apartment, get enough insurance to cover the value of your possessions.

Chapter 12

Roomies

With a roommate you could afford a much bigger or nicer place than you can rent by yourself. But roommates can really be a pain if you're not careful in your choice. What kind of roommate are you? Answer these questions to find out. Download this questionnaire at http://www.simonsays.com/content/book.cfm?tab=1&pid=614860&agid=38.

1. How clean do you keep your room?

   Very Somewhat Total Slob

2. How clean do you keep your bathroom?

   Very So-so Only when Mom's visiting

3. How clean do you keep your kitchen?

   Very Decent I don't do dishes

4. What kind of music do you like? ____________________

5. How do you like your music?

   No music—ever   Music as background   Occasionally   I rock out

6. How often do you have guests?

   Never   Two or three times a week   Weekends only   Daily

7. How often are you away?

   Never   Once in a while   Weekly   Monthly

8. When do you take showers?

   Morning   Evening   Rarely

9. Do you have overnight guests?

   Yes   No   Of the opposite sex?   Yes   No

10. Do you mind if people borrow your stuff?

    Yes   No

11. Do you borrow other people's stuff?

    Yes   No

12. Do you sleep with your music or TV on or off? __________

13. How many hours of sleep do you need per night?

    More then 8   8   6   Sleep, who needs sleep?

14. When should be the time for lights-out?

    10 p.m.   11 p.m.   Midnight   Never

15. Do you need a set quiet time each day to study/work?

    Yes   No   If so, when? __________________

16. Do you throw parties?

    Never   Once in a while   Every weekend   Every night

17. Do you set the alarm on weekends?

    Yes No

18. Are you a talker or nontalker? ____________________

19. Do you need to have people around or do you need your space?

20. How do you handle conflict?

    Tell friends Steam Explode Confront

After you've completed the quiz, have your potential roommate take it as well. Talk about it over a latte. Communication is the key to being a good roommate.

While you're talking, here are some other topics to discuss:

- Who's paying for what?
- How are you going to share food/the kitchen?
- Do either of you have any medical concerns or allergies?
- How will you communicate with each other when a problem comes up?
- Should you worry if your roommate doesn't come home at night?

Chapter 13

Treaties and Truces

The best way to avoid problems with roommates is to anticipate them and work out the solutions beforehand. Using a roommate treaty like the one below puts things on paper so each of you is clear about your responsibilities and the other person's expectations.

Roommate treaty

Roomie 1 ______________________________

Roomie 2 ______________________________

Address ______________________________

Lease dates ______________________________

Rent per month ____________ Rent due date ____________

1. Rent

__________________________ agrees to pay $ ____________ toward rent each month, not later than ________________________.

__________________________ agrees to pay $________ toward rent each month, not later than ____________________________.

2. Utilities—electricity, heating, water, sewer, garbage removal, cable, telephone, etc.

__________________________ agrees to pay the following bills every month: ____

____

____

__________________________ agrees to pay the following bills every month: ____

____

____

__________________________ and __________________________ agree to split the following bills equally each month: ________________

____

____

____

3. Bedrooms

__________________________ will occupy ______________ bedroom.

__________________________ will occupy ______________ bedroom.

4. Food, kitchen, and cooking

We will/will not share all food.
We will/will not share cooking duties.
We agree to share the following food items: ____________

We agree not to share the following food items: ____________

____________ will be responsible for buying ____

____________.

____________ will be responsible for buying ____

____________.

5. Cleaning

____________ and ____________ agree to share housecleaning chores.

We agree that we each are responsible for cleaning our own bedrooms, private baths, and other private rooms.
We agree that we will share the responsibility for cleaning common areas, such as the kitchen, living area, shared bath, deck/patio.
____________ will be responsible for the following chores: ____________

____________.

____________ will be responsible for the following chores: ____________

____________.

We agree to alternate (daily/weekly/monthly) doing the following chores: ____________

____

____

____

6. Overnight guests

____________________ and __________________ have agreed that it is ______________________ to have guests spend the night.

Food for guests will be provided by ______________________.

Guests need to leave by _______ on weekdays and _______ on weekends.

Additional comments/specifications: ______________________

____

____

7. Quiet time

We agree that lights and audible media will be turned off by __________ at night.

We agree that from _____________ to _______ will be quiet hours during the week and from ________ to _______ on weekends.

8. Parking

_______________________ will park ______________________.

_______________________ will park ______________________.

9. Disagreements

If at any time we disagree or dislike the action of the other, we promise to talk to each other before we talk to anyone else. We promise to listen to each other and try to work out a solution together.

If, for any reason, either of us wants/needs to move out, we agree to give _____________________ days' notice. Any owed rent or utilities will be paid before we leave.

Signature of Roomie 1 ____________________ Date________

Signature of Roomie 2 ____________________ Date________

Chapter 14

Purchasing Your First Home

Do you dream of owning a little country cottage with roses trailing up a white picket fence? Or perhaps purchasing a loft downtown. Whatever the dream, the reality is that buying a home will be one of, if not the one, biggest purchase of your life. To make that dream a reality demands much planning on your part.

Steps to take NOW if you want to purchase a home sometime in your life

- Stay out of debt. If you have any debt, pay it off.
- Keep a high credit score.
- Save money.
- Build a consistent employment record. Banks are leery of loaning money to someone without a stable source of income.

How much money does it take to buy a home?

- *Down payment:* The ideal down payment is 20 percent of the purchase price. This means that if you purchase a $150,000 house, your down payment would be $30,000.
- *Closing costs:* These are fees you have to pay when you close your mortgage. Most fees are based on the purchase price of the home.
- *Escrow fees:* $400–$1,200. This covers administrative costs of preparing your loan.
- *Homeowners insurance:* $300–$1500. You have to pay the first year's premium in advance.
- *Title insurance:* $300–$1000
- *Property tax:* The amount depends on the value of your home plus the time of year purchased.
- *Legal fees:* $300–$600
- *Inspections:* $250–$600

Not just a home—an investment

More than likely, the first home you purchase will not be your last. Don't go looking for your dream home the first time out. Instead, look at the home as an investment.

Say you find a sturdy home with lots of potential in an area where homes sell fairly quickly. You buy it, financing $100,000 of the purchase price. Over the next two years you clean, paint, and replace some appliances—an investment of your time plus $5,000. Then you sell the house for $150,000. After expenses and real estate fees, you walk away with about $35,000 plus the amount of your down payment and any principal you paid on your loan. Now you have a decent down payment for your next home.

- *Private Mortgage Insurance (PMI):* $200–$500. This insurance is required if your down payment is less than 20 percent.
- *Prepaid loan interest:* This is the interest accrued between closing and when your first payment is due. This is why it's always better to close at the end of the month.
- *Recording:* Around $50
- *Notary:* $20–$60

Bottom line: You'll need to have about $33,000 saved in order to purchase a $150,000 home.

Saving is not impossible!

If you were to put aside $500 a month for five years in an account earning 6 percent interest, you'll have $35,559 in the bank.

House-hunting tips

- Know what you can afford.
- Be pretty certain you're going to live in the house longer than two years.
- Study the neighborhood.
- It is much better to buy the cheapest, ugliest house in a neighborhood with good schools and a low crime rate than to purchase the most expensive house in an area with poor schools and high crime.
- Look at your first house as an investment, not as your dream house.
- Be realistic about how much work and money you can or will put into a home that needs renovation or improvement.

What can you afford?

The mortgage payment, property taxes, and homeowner's insurance should be less than 28 percent of your gross income. If you make $3,000 a month (before taxes), your total house costs should be less than $840 per month.

Remember: in some areas property taxes drastically increase your monthly house payment.

- Go house-browsing before you get a Realtor. Look, don't buy!
- Visit open houses and model homes. Take notes on what you like and don't like. Ask lots of questions. Research houses on the Web. Notice how long houses in different areas of town stay on the market before they sell.

Mistakes to avoid

- Letting a Realtor sway you into purchasing more house than you can afford.
- Offering the listing price. Always make your first offer 8 to 10 percent below the asking price.
- Buying a house and not reserving money to furnish it or do anything else.
- Looking at just one mortgage provider. Shop around and compare.
- Not getting preapproved for a mortgage.
- Purchasing a house without having it inspected by a professional. The last thing you want is to find out you need a new roof after you've purchased the home.
- Not asking about covenants or restrictions.

Why a down payment of 20 percent?

Let's say you get transferred to a new job site the week after you close on your house and you need to put the house up for sale right away. The value of the property has not gone up, so you can only sell it for the $150,000 you paid (and you might have to settle for less). The Realtor's fee is typically around 7 percent, so you'll already be out $10,500—not to mention the mortgage fees, cost of a home inspection, etc. You might lose most of your down payment, but by putting down 20 percent, hopefully you won't owe anything if you have to sell your house in the first year or two.

House homework sheet

First, consult with a couple of mortgage companies and determine an affordable price range. (See chapter 15.) Be realistic in counting the cost. Remember, you'll want to buy furniture and have a life after you purchase your home. You can download all of the following worksheets at http://www.simonsays.com/content/book.cfm?tab=1&pid=614860&agid=38.

My maximum purchase price: ______________________________

Potential neighborhoods, subdivisions, or streets: ______________

____

____

Minimum number of bedrooms: ___________________________

Minimum number of bathrooms: __________________________

Parking needs: ☐ garage ☐ off street # of cars ________

Other needs: ____

____

House-/condo-hunting worksheets

Download this online form at http://www.simonsays.com/content/book.cfm?tab=1&pid=614860&agid=38

Neighborhood/subdivision/building: ______________________

Address: ______________________________________

MLS #: ________________Time on market: ____________

Distance from work/school: __________________________

Interior features

How many square feet: _______

Space needed: ______________ # of bedrooms: __________

# of bathrooms: ____________ # of closets: ____________

Check all that apply:

- ☐ shower
- ☐ dishwasher
- ☐ good water pressure
- ☐ microwave
- ☐ adequate lighting
- ☐ locks on doors
- ☐ handicap accessible
- ☐ fire extinguishers
- ☐ smoke detectors
- ☐ bathtub
- ☐ laundry hookups
- ☐ air conditioning
- ☐ refrigerator
- ☐ window blinds
- ☐ good cell-phone reception
- ☐ Internet access
- ☐ additional storage
- ☐ well-maintained/clean

List age of the following:

House: _________ Roof:_________ Furnace: ____________

Air conditioner: _______________ Appliances: __________

List other pros: ______________________________

List any cons: ______________________________

Exterior features

- ☐ laundry facility
- ☐ parking lot
- ☐ security system/doorman
- ☐ safe neighborhood
- ☐ near grocery store
- ☐ fenced yard
- ☐ gym
- ☐ good schools
- ☐ mailbox
- ☐ garage
- ☐ well-lighted exterior
- ☐ near mass transit
- ☐ yard
- ☐ pool
- ☐ garbage removal/ Dumpster
- ☐ well-maintained/clean

If a condo, is it on the first floor? ____________________

What is the noise level? ______________________________

What is the condition of neighboring houses? ______________

____

First-floor pros and cons

First-floor apartments or condos have their pros and cons:

- Pro: easier access for you.
- Con: easier access for someone trying to break in.
- Con: noise level (you hear all the action outside since you are at ground level).
- Pro: You won't bother your neighbors if you're in the habit of doing aerobics or running in place every morning at five a.m.

Chapter 15

Your First Mortgage

You compare prices on items you want to buy, in order to find a good deal—and shopping for mortgages should be no exception. You could save thousands of dollars by doing a little research. However, be sure to look at the total cost of your loan, not just the up-front costs, when making your decision.

Types of mortgages

- ***Fixed-rate mortgage:*** Interest rate stays the same for the length of the mortgage.
- ***Adjustable-rate mortgage:*** Interest starts at one rate and then adjusts to current market rate after a predetermined time. Mortgage payment will change along with the interest rate.

- ***Balloon mortgage:*** Interest rate set for predetermined amount of time. You must refinance your mortgage after that time has expired.
- ***Interest-only mortgage:*** You pay escrow payments plus interest on your loan for a set number of years. During this time none of your payments go toward the principal, so the amount you owe on the loan stays the same.

Truth in lending

Your mortgage company is required to provide you with a Truth in Lending Disclosure Statement within three days of your loan application. This statement provides you with valuable information, such as the estimated total cost of borrowing and expected monthly payments. Read it with care.

What is PMI?

Private Mortgage Insurance (PMI) is required by lenders when a loan is originated and closed without a 20 percent down payment. This insurance protects the lender from default losses in the event a loan becomes delinquent.[2]

Getting preapproved for a mortgage does two things:

1. It lets you know how much house you can afford and that you really can buy a house.
2. It lets the Realtor and seller know that not only are you serious about buying a house, you also have the finances to do so.

Comparing mortgages

Use the worksheet below to compare mortgage loans and companies. You can download this worksheet at http://www.simonsays.com/content/book.cfm?tab=1&pid=614860&agid=38.

Name of lender			
Contact, phone number			
Mortgage amount			
Type of loan			
Minimum down payment			
Length of loan			
Interest rate			
Annual percentage rate			
Points			
PMI premiums			
How long you have to keep PMI			
Estimated monthly escrow			
Estimated total monthly house payment			
Application/loan processing fee			

Origination/underwriting fee			
Lender/funding fee			
Appraisal fee			
Attorney fee			
Document preparation and recording fees			
Broker fees			
Credit report fees			
Other fees			
Title search/ title insurance			
Estimated prepaid amounts for interest, taxes, insurances, escrow payments			
Taxes			
Flood determination			
Surveys and home inspections			
Total fee and closing cost estimates			

Understand what you're really paying

Look at the difference between a fifteen-and thirty-year mortgage of $150,000, each at a 6 percent interest rate.

Type of mortgage	15-year fixed	30-year fixed
Monthly payment (not including taxes or insurance)	$1,265.79	$899.33
Interest paid over 10 years	$67,695.06	$84,075.32
Amount still owed after 10 years	$64,535.03	$125,256.90
Amount owed after 15 years	$0 Nothing, nada, zip	$106,206.81

PART 4

GOD AND ME

Embracing your faith as your own is a major step into adulthood. What do you want your relationship with God to look like? Do you want no relationship with Him? Do you want one that is "Sundays only"? Or do you want to know God on a personal and intimate level?

As with any relationship, the time, effort, and priority you place on it will influence the level of intimacy.

Chapter 16

Making Time for God

What could be better than a fresh doughnut? But leave that tasty pastry on the counter, and a day later it's stale and dried out. A week later, if mold hasn't started growing on it, you have a nice paperweight. Give it a month, and you have a hockey puck.

God is gracious, but to really keep your relationship with Him fresh, spending time with Him each day is ideal. God desires us to talk with Him every day. In your busy new adult life, that can be hard to do . . . unless you have a plan. Just as you have a work schedule or class schedule, it's a good idea to schedule daily time with God.

God doesn't really dictate what that time with Him has to look like, but here are some suggestions to help you get started.

In your home

- Before you get out of bed to start your day, talk to God.
- Designate a place for your time with God—for example a comfy couch or a chair on the deck.
- Along with your Bible, bring a journal to record your thoughts and what you think God is teaching you.
- Subscribe to an online Bible-reading or devotional program that e-mails readings to you daily.

What is "quiet time"?

We often think of "quiet time" as a time for daily Bible reading. But this can also be your time to worship, with all the aspects of worship you have participated in during more corporate settings. You can include music, prayer, and praise, as well as Bible study.

On the go

- Put an audio version of the Bible on your iPod or MP3 player. Listen while you're walking somewhere or exercising. Dramatic readings often bring new energy into familiar stories.
- Download or subscribe to podcasts of great preaching or teaching, and listen to them while you're on the go.
- Store a text version of the Bible on your laptop or BlackBerry. This allows you to read Scripture in those unexpected quiet moments, like while you're waiting in the doctor's office or during a break between classes.

Your goals with God's time

I purpose to spend __________ time with God every __________ .
What I would like my personal worship to look like: __________

____

Things I would like to ask God: ______________________

____

____

Things I would like to study about God: ________________

____

____

Books of the Bible I have never read but would like to: _______

____

Recommended devotional resources

(For friends or family members to fill out)

What has worked for me: __________________________

____

____

Books that impacted my faith life: ____________________

____

____

What has worked for me: __________________________

____

____

Books that impacted my faith life: ____________________

____

____

Sample spiritual journal

Date ____

I give thanks for ________________________________.

This part of God's character blew me away today: ____________

____.

I confess____

____.

I'll pray for these people/needs today: _________________

____.

Today I read______________________________________

What I learned or what struck me most was ______________

____.

What I need to apply is ____________________________

____.

I'm going to apply it to my life by ____________________

____.

My closing thought or prayer is _______________________

____

____

____.

Suggested Bible resources

- Study Bible with notes and reference material
- One-year chronological Bible (passages arranged as they unfolded in history)
- Bible Reading Plans (www.bibleplan.org)
- Blue Letter Bible (www.blueletterbible.org)
- Crosswalk.com (www.bible.crosswalk.com)
- BibleGateway.com

Chapter 17

Your Church

God has designed us to be part of a family . . . His family. By definition, family life is not an individual experience. Something sacred happens when we worship God together, not just on Sunday mornings but through shared prayer, service, and encouragement 24/7. God pours out His love and comfort through community.

The goal of this chapter is to help you find a church community you can call home.

Five signs of a healthy church

1. *Preaching and prayer*—Do preaching and prayer have priority? Look for preaching that

is authentic, challenging, expectant, and uses the Bible as the authoritative text. Are prayer requests transparent and personal?

"*[We] will give our attention to prayer and the ministry of the word*" (Acts 6:4).

2. *Love*—Does loving each other have equal priority? Is it a safe place? Do people encourage or criticize?

   "*By this all men will know that you are my disciples, if you love one another*" (John 13:35).

3. *Participation*—Are all attendees being equipped and encouraged to use their unique gifts? Do volunteers receive training? Are gift assessment and placement programs available?

   "*It was he who gave some to be apostles, some to be prophets, some to be evangelists, and some to be pastors and teachers, to prepare God's people for works of service, so that the body of Christ may be built up*" (Ephesians 4:11–12).

4. *Missions*—Does the church value reaching out to others through evangelism, missions, and church planting? Are mission opportunities available, both long- and short-term, locally and abroad?

   "*Go and make disciples of all nations, baptizing them in the name of the Father and of the Son and of the Holy Spirit*" (Matthew 28:19).

5. *Meeting needs*—Does the church come alongside those in need, especially widows and the fatherless? Are single people involved in the church? Does the church minister to people in crisis?

"If anyone has material possessions and sees his brother in need but has no pity on him, how can the love of God be in him?" (1 John 3:17)

Remember, forgiven people fill the church, not perfect ones

"Let us consider how we may spur one another on toward love and good deeds. Let us not give up meeting together, as some are in the habit of doing, but let us encourage one another—and all the more as you see the Day approaching" (Hebrews 10: 24–25).

Your ideal church

Write down your preference for each item, then rank them by importance.

Church denomination/theology

Preference ______________________________ Priority________

Church size

Preference ______________________________ Priority________

Worship style

Preference ______________________________ Priority________

Ministries/activities

Preference ______________________________ Priority________

Preaching style

Preference ______________________________ Priority________

Opportunities to serve

Preference ______________________________ Priority ________

Church-search tips

- When looking for a church, first pray that God will lead you to the right place.
- The Internet is a great way to research local churches even before you leave home.
- Don't be afraid to check out more than one church, but don't judge a church by one visit. We're all allowed to have an off day!

Potential churches

Before you visit potential churches, download this form at http://www.simonsays.com/content/book.cfm?tab=1&pid=614860&agid=38 and be sure to fill out the following information for each church so you can remember specific things about each one you visit.

Church name ________________________________

Pastor ____________________ Phone ____________________

Address ________________________________

Web site ________________________________

E-mail ________________________________

Date visited ________________ Service times ______________

I have read and agree with their Statement of Faith.
☐ Yes ☐ Haven't read it ☐ Have read it but don't agree
Comments ________________________________

____

____

If this church is less than ideal, is it a place you could worship, fellowship, and grow spiritually? ☐ yes ☐ no

Other Christian organizations for young adults

- Campus Crusade for Christ International (www.ccci.org)
- The Navigators (www.navigators.org)
- Reformed University Fellowship (www.ruf.org)
- Notreligion.com
- Focus on the Family (boundless.org)

Chapter 18

Your Church, Your Part

"The notion of people belonging to the church in order to come to sit down and fold their arms and listen, with just two or three doing everything, is quite foreign to the New Testament."

—D. Martyn Lloyd-Jones

What does it mean to be a grown-up member of a church? Perhaps you've grown up in the church, and your experience to this point has been that of a child. Perhaps you've never gone to church. Either way, you may be uncertain about what's involved in being an adult in a church family. Below are some tips on doing your part in your church:

- Love and encourage one another —in good times and in bad.

- If you have a problem or conflict, always go first to the person with whom you have an issue. Give the person a chance to explain his or her actions or the circumstances.
- Pray regularly for the entire church body.
- Participate: It's awfully hard to build a relationship with God or others if you're not interacting with them.
- Support your church through the giving of your time, talents, and finances. Churches get a bad rap for asking for money. But the fact is that utilities, insurance, salaries, and coffee all cost money. You can also save the church money by volunteering to assist in the church office, provide child care, or do landscaping or janitorial work.

Chapter 19

What Isn't a Church

Cults are spiritual groups that manipulate their members for gain. Don Veinot identified the following hallmarks of a cult:

- The leadership claims to be sent by God to "rule" the one true religion.
- Cult members must believe exactly the same way and in exactly the same things.

Warning signs that a religious group may be a cult

- Leader is always 100 percent right.
- Encourages isolation from family and friends.
- Group will not disclose finances.
- Members show unreasonable fear about the outside world.

For more warning signs, visit www.rickross.com/warningsigns.html.

- Cults claim they've been given a "special revelation" from God that is superior to the Bible.
- Cults often depict basic Christian doctrine and belief as full of holes.
- Bible verses are often taken out of context or twisted.
- Cult members believe God has given their group the job of pointing out "heretical and evil" teachings of Christianity.
- Cult members say their works prove their religion is the one and only truth.
- Cults often teach that salvation is based on performance, so cult members can never know if they've done everything necessary to get to heaven.
- Leaving a cult is not an option. Intimidation is often used to keep cult members from even thinking about getting out.[3]

PART 5
OTHER RELATIONSHIPS

"It is not good for the man to be alone," God stated in Genesis 2:18. In fact, we can only give or receive certain things within the context of a relationship with others—things like love, encouragement, sympathy, kindness, hospitality, empathy, and comfort.

However, the quality of our relationships matters more than our quantity of friends. As Paul said in 1 Corinthians, "Bad company corrupts good character." Developing healthy relationships with admirable individuals* will help nurture your own good gifts and personality traits as well as help curb those not-so-wonderful tendencies.

*Am I saying you shouldn't hang around "sinners"? No, that would be contrary to Jesus' own teachings. Obviously, we are to show and share the love of God with everyone. What I'm saying is that to maintain your character in a world full of temptations, it's important that your core friendships encourage your personal best.

Chapter 20

Creating Community

Your community is made up of the people you hang out with. People in your community could be coworkers, roommates, classmates, teammates, or people you attend church or Bible study with.

The purpose of community is to have a group of people who encourage, support, and love one another. Community is not just about meeting your own needs but about meeting the needs of those around you. You'll want a community that brings out the best in you—one that pushes you forward, strengthens you character, and lifts you up.

Now that you've moved away from family and childhood friends, you'll need to develop a new group of friends—a new community. Your community can be large or small, though having a community of only one other person is never a healthy situation.

So how do you go about creating community? It does require some initiative. Think first about what type of community you want to be part of. Write down your thoughts:

____

____

____

____

____

____

____

Now write down where you could meet the kind of people you'd want to be part of your community:

____

____

____

Next, plan an activity to which you can invite a group of people (a group is anything more than one other person).

After that activity takes place, plan another event and invite the same group of people. This is important. Community isn't established at a one-time event. It takes time and interaction to develop relationships.

Building Friendships

Building a group of friends is something you can initiate, but it's not something you can force. A good rule of thumb: Invite people to two different events. If they don't show, let them go.

A little nervous? That's okay. The next two chapters will cover how to host an event and give you some ideas on what to do.

Chapter 21

The Host(ess) with the Most(est)

The goal of a host or hostess is to make guests feel comfortable. Here are some tips for how to make that happen:

- Your guests will be as relaxed as you are, so plan an event that won't stress you out. Keep it simple.
- Provide at least two choices of soft drinks, including one diet drink.
- Food always makes people happy. Have plenty on hand, but don't overdo it.
- When hosting a coed event, make sure you have at least three

men and three women; otherwise it feels too much like a double date.

- Introduce each new arrival to the group. Share a couple of things about the person (be sure to keep it positive). (Example: "Hey, guys, this is Sam. He plays a mean game of basketball.") Little bits of information like this give people a conversation starter.
- Have background music playing. The volume should be low enough that people can talk to each other but loud enough to cover any awkward moments of silence.
- Make sure you mingle and spend time talking with each of your guests.
- If you plan for something specific to happen at your activity, like serving birthday cake, watching a movie, or eating a meal, let people know what time this event will begin. (Example: "Come over anytime after six o'clock to hang out. I was thinking we'd start the movie around seven.")
- If you don't want people hanging around your place all night, let them know in advance what your expectations are. (Example: "Hey, let's get together and play some cards tomorrow, say from eight to ten. Okay?")
- Give a clue as to appropriate dress. Sometimes the clue will be inherent in your invitation: if you're planning to go to a ball game or for a hike, people will automatically know how to dress. But if you're hosting a party or dinner, let people know whether it's casual (as in, "We're ordering pizza, so T-shirts and jeans are just fine") or more formal (for example, if it's a themed party and calls for themed dress, or if it's a candlelight dinner and the person who shows up in sweats might feel underdressed).

Good foods to have on hand for gatherings

- Popcorn
- Chips and salsa (Put these in bowls for your guests—no eating out of the bag or jar.)
- Nuts
- Carrots and dip
- At least two types of soft drink, one being diet
- Coffee/tea
- Bottled water
- M&M's

Chapter 22

Fun, Exciting, Cheap, and Legal Things to Do

You can host an activity at your home or at another location. Here are some ideas for both.

At home

- *Movie night*—Rent a movie; provide popcorn and soft drinks.
- *Game night*—Play cards or board games; provide snacks and soft drinks. For card game ideas and rules, visit www.pagat.com or www.usplayingcard.com.
- *Pizza night*—Either take a collection to have some delivered or make homemade pizza as a group.
- *Picnic on the floor (great for a winter day)*—Provide blanket, sandwiches, chips, cookies, and drinks.

- *Book club or Bible study*—Individuals read a specific book (chosen and agreed upon in advance), then meet to discuss what they've read. Provide coffee/tea and M&M's.
- *Craft night*—Do anything crafty, from knitting or scrapbooking to painting pet rocks. Have everyone bring his or her own supplies; you provide snacks and drinks.
- *Creative evening*—This is a grown-up version of show-and-tell. If you hang with creative-type people, have them bring something they've created, like a painting, photograph, poem, etc. In addition, you can tape a large piece of paper to a wall and provide everyone with crayons to color a mural.
- *Sports night*—Watch a game and eat pizza.

Away from home

- Go bowling.
- Go to a movie.
- Plan an "upside-down dinner." Go to three or four different restaurants: at the first order one or two desserts to share; at the next a main dish; at the next appetizers.
- Volunteer or do a service project together (see chapter 60 for ideas).
- Attend church together.
- Go to a cultural event, like a concert or a play.
- Attend a local sporting event.
- Meet at a park and play ultimate Frisbee, football, or some other sport.
- Take a day trip and do some local sightseeing.

Tradition

Traditions serve as glue in relationships. Traditions also can set one community apart from another. They're what make your group unique and special.

Now that you're away from home, take time to create some traditions of your own (nothing elaborate or expensive, as you'll want to be able to maintain the tradition over time). Here are some ideas for new traditions:

- Rent an old movie once a month and have friends over for pizza.
- Have a Sabbath dinner on Saturday nights with a group of friends.
- Have an Everyday Thanksgiving. At any shared meal, ask those you are eating with to name one thing they're thankful for.
- Play flag football on Labor Day.
- Pack a picnic and see fireworks on the Fourth of July.
- Take a road trip together once a year.

Chapter 23

When Sad Is Bad

Every two hours, a young person between the ages of fifteen and twenty-four commits suicide in the United States, and for every suicide there are one hundred to two hundred attempts.[4] As a friend, you need to be aware of the following warning signs and take any suicide threats seriously.

Warning signs

According to the Ohio Coalition for Suicide Prevention, early warning signs may include the following:

- Changes in eating or sleeping habits
- Apathy about school or job interests
- Outbursts of anger, mood swings, and drastic changes in behavior

- Withdrawal from family, friends, and social activities
- Increased use of alcohol and drugs
- Recent loss, such as the death of a loved one, breakup of a relationship, or loss of a job
- Preoccupation with death
- Giving away prized possessions
- Making final arrangements, such as wills, funeral plans, and insurance changes
- Direct and indirect statements (e.g., "I wish I were dead")
- Previous suicide attempts[5]

What to do if a friend is suicidal

Ask them

- Are you thinking about dying?
- Are you thinking about hurting yourself?
- Are you thinking about suicide?
- Have you thought about how you would do it?
- Do you know when you would do it?
- Do you have the means to do it?[6]

Call

- 911 if the person is in immediate danger
- National Suicide Prevention Lifeline, 1-800-273-TALK (8255)
- National Hopeline, 1-800-SUICIDE (784-2433)

Get help

You are a friend, not a mental health expert. If danger is imminent, call 911. If the threat is not imminent, work with your friend to find professional medical or counseling help. People who are seriously depressed will need a friend to help motivate them to get the help they need.

DO NOT

- Do not promise you will keep the person's thoughts a secret. You want your friend to trust you, and this is a promise you cannot keep.
- Do not put yourself in harm's way. If a friend calls you and tells you he or she is about to commit suicide, call 911 immediately. Do not go to your friend's house by yourself.

Remember

You are not responsible for your friend's actions. You are only responsible for your own. Take the steps necessary to get the person assistance. But if your friend takes his or her own life, it's not your fault.

Chapter 24

When You're More Than Just Friends

Most Americans get married between the ages of twenty-five and twenty-six. That being said, you are at a point in your life when you're likely to develop a relationship with the person you're going to marry. Scary, huh?

Okay, so you've met someone and are wondering if he or she is "the one." Maybe taking a relationship inventory will help clarify the situation.

Each of you should complete it separately—meaning at different times and places. No looking over each other's shoulders or coaching answers. Plan a time to discuss your answers together. Do this before you get engaged!

Relationship inventory

1. I would describe my boyfriend/girlfriend as
   - ☐ someone I can tolerate for long periods of time.
   - ☐ someone I can live with.
   - ☐ someone I can't live without.

2. I can serve the Lord better
   - ☐ with this person.
   - ☐ by remaining single.

3. Check all that describe you:
   - ☐ introvert
   - ☐ extrovert
   - ☐ affectionate
   - ☐ not affectionate
   - ☐ have lots of friends
   - ☐ have a small group of friends
   - ☐ have no friends at all
   - ☐ talker
   - ☐ nontalker
   - ☐ leader
   - ☐ follower
   - ☐ loner
   - ☐ need to be out and about
   - ☐ like staying at home

4. In five years, I see myself
   - ☐ working hard at building my career.
   - ☐ still in school.
   - ☐ at home, taking care of kids full time.
   - ☐ exploring the world, taking odd jobs to support myself.

- ☐ living with my parents.
- ☐ (other) ______________________________.

5. My career is
   - ☐ very important to me. I will do everything it takes to advance my career.
   - ☐ important to me. I expect to work full time and want to succeed.
   - ☐ flexible. I will defer to my spouse's career.
   - ☐ not important. I will work when and where I have to.
   - ☐ temporary and/or something I'll pursue later. I plan to work outside the home but would like to stay at home while raising children.
   - ☐ nonexistent. I don't expect to work.

6. I think sex is
   - ☐ a vital part of a healthy marriage but is for marriage only.
   - ☐ a natural part of any serious boy/girl relationship, whether you're married or not.
   - ☐ fun with anyone.
   - ☐ embarrassing and gross.

7. I think the ideal family size includes
   - ☐ no children.
   - ☐ one child.
   - ☐ two children.
   - ☐ three children.
   - ☐ four children.
   - ☐ five or more children.

8. In regard to money, I
   - ☐ am very financially conservative: I save most of what I learn.

- ☐ like to both save and spend money but am uncomfortable with any debt.*
- ☐ spend everything I earn but have no debt.
- ☐ have a minimal amount of debt and plan to work extra jobs in order to pay it off quickly.
- ☐ am in debt up to my eyeballs.

9. Financially speaking, I have
   - ☐ a nice amount tucked away in savings/investments and no debt.
   - ☐ a small amount of savings and no debt.
   - ☐ no savings and less then $1,000 in debt.
   - ☐ between $2,000 and $5,000 in debt.
   - ☐ between $6,000 and $10,000 in debt.
   - ☐ over $10,000 in debt.

10. I would like to live
    - ☐ in a major city.
    - ☐ in the suburbs of a major city.
    - ☐ in a midsize city.
    - ☐ in a small town.
    - ☐ in a rural setting.
    - ☐ in the wilderness.
    - ☐ on the beach.
    - ☐ in a foreign country.

11. My faith is
    - ☐ a very important part of my life.
    - ☐ a somewhat important part of my life.
    - ☐ not a critical part of my life.
    - ☐ not part of my life at all.

*For this questionnaire, debt includes all credit cards, student loans, car loans, mortgages on rental properties, and second mortgages. It does not include a first mortgage on your primary residence.

12. I think attending church is
    - ☐ something you should do at least once a week.
    - ☐ something you should do two to three times a month.
    - ☐ something you should do on holidays, like Easter or Christmas.
    - ☐ stupid. I will never attend a church.

13. As a couple, I expect us to
    - ☐ make our faith the center of our family life.
    - ☐ practice our faith on Sundays only.
    - ☐ practice our faiths separately.
    - ☐ not practice any faith.

14. My parents and siblings are
    - ☐ so important that I could never move away from them.
    - ☐ a major part of my life. I expect to spend every holiday with them.
    - ☐ an important part of my life. I would like to spend some holidays with them.
    - ☐ an important part of my life, but I don't need to visit them on holidays.
    - ☐ annoying. I only want to speak to them occasionally.
    - ☐ awful. I don't want anything to do with my family.

15. If I could change one thing about my boyfriend/girlfriend, it would be ______________________________

    ____

    ____

16. Can I see this person as the mother/father of my children?

    ☐ Yes ☐ No

17. I feel that my boyfriend/girlfriend
    - ☐ is very supportive and loves me for who I am.
    - ☐ likes me most of the time but would like to change some things about me.
    - ☐ doesn't trust me.
    - ☐ is only settling for me because he/she can't find anyone better at the moment.
    - ☐ disagrees with almost everything I do.

18. I view marriage as
    - ☐ a forever deal.
    - ☐ good, until I am unhappy.
    - ☐ unnecessary.

19. I would like to get married some day so that
    - ☐ someone will take care of me.
    - ☐ I can help and support my spouse.
    - ☐ I can be happy.
    - ☐ I can build a lifelong relationship with the person I love most.
    - ☐ I can start a family.

20. When I'm not working, I like to
    - ☐ watch TV or play video games.
    - ☐ do housework or yard work.
    - ☐ be on the computer.
    - ☐ talk to someone.
    - ☐ go out and do something.
    - ☐ read a book.
    - ☐ have friends over.
    - ☐ (other) ______________________________.

21. When I think about getting married to my boyfriend/girlfriend, I
    - ☐ can't stop smiling.
    - ☐ am a little nervous.
    - ☐ feel sick to my stomach.

22. Is there anything in Scripture that would speak against my marrying this person? ☐ yes ☐ no

23. My future in-laws
    - ☐ know and accept me.
    - ☐ don't know me yet.
    - ☐ hate my guts.
    - ☐ don't care.

24. Can I see myself as part of my boyfriend's/girlfriend's family? ☐ yes ☐ no

25. The people who know me best think that my boyfriend/girlfriend and I getting married would be
    - ☐ the best thing that could ever happen to me.
    - ☐ okay, but they have some reservations.
    - ☐ a totally bad idea.

26. Do I feel safe talking to my boyfriend/girlfriend about difficult things? ☐ yes ☐ no

A case for abstinence

Why not be sexually active before marriage? Any sexual contact, including oral sex and kissing, puts you at risk of getting a sexually transmitted disease (STD). Most STDs have no symptoms—but they have very serious consequences. Before you get hot and heavy with someone, you may want to look at the following chart.

STD	How you can get it	Symptoms	Complications
Chlamydia	Sex, including oral sex	In 75 percent of people, no symptoms; symptoms include burning sensation during urination and discharge from penis, vagina, or rectum	• Pelvic inflammatory disease • Chronic pelvic pain • Infertility (in women) • Sterility (in men)
Bacterial vaginosis	Any contact with penis, mouth, vagina, or anus	Discharge, pain, itching	• Pelvic inflammatory disease • Complications in pregnancy • Increased chance of getting HIV/AIDS
Gonorrhea	Any contact with penis, vagina, mouth, or anus	For most people, no or very mild symptoms, including burning and pain while urinating, discharge from penis or vagina, sore throat	• Pelvic inflammatory disease, infertility, sterility • In babies: blindness, joint infection, life-threatening blood infection
Hepatitis B (no cure)	Sexual contact, drug use, sharing toothbrushes or razors	For many people, no symptoms; symptoms include fatigue, low-grade fever, nausea, joint aches, jaundice	• Chronic infections • Cirrhosis, liver cancer, liver failure, death

Herpes (no cure)	Sexual contact, including oral sex	For many people, no symptoms; symptoms include fever, blisters in genital area, muscle aches	• Recurrent painful genital sores • In babies: fatal infections
HIV/AIDS (no cure)	Sex, including oral sex, plus drug use and blood transfusions	No symptoms for 1–2 months, then flulike symptoms	Chronic illness, coma, cancer, death
Human papillomavirus (HPV)	Genital contact	For most people, no symptoms; symptoms include raised, flesh-colored lesions on genitals, cauliflower-like growths around genitals, genital itching, vaginal discharge	Cervical cancer
Syphilis	Sex, including oral sex	No symptoms for years	• Damaged brain, heart, eyes, bones • Paralysis • Death
Trichomoniasis	Sexual contact	For some people, no symptoms; others experience discharge	• Increased risk of getting HIV/AIDS • Babies born with complications

Who are you really sleeping with?

When you have sexual contact with someone (including kissing, fondling, oral sex, anal sex, and vaginal sex), remember that you are exposing yourself to the diseases carried by any of his or her previous partners.

A case for purity

Abstinence is about avoiding sex, thus shielding you from sexual consequences and sin. Purity is about focusing your whole self on the beauty and majesty of our Lord Jesus Christ and agreeing with Him that a lifelong, committed, faithful, loving, intimate, monogamous relationship between one man and one woman is the standard. It's about understanding that God wants you to have that kind of pure relationship with Him as well as with your spouse.

Consider what God's Word says about being pure: "It is God's will that you should be sanctified: that you should avoid sexual immorality; that each of you should learn to control his own body in a way that is holy and honorable, not in passionate lust like the heathen, who do not know God; and that in this matter no one should wrong his brother or take advantage of him" (1 Thessalonians 4:3–6).

Truth is, purity plays a role in all your relationships.

Loving and respecting God

To love God is to obey His commands. God created sex as a happy and good thing to be enjoyed by a husband and wife. Respecting God means acknowledging that God knew what He was talking about when He made the rules. He set up boundaries around sex for the protection of you, others, and your future children.

Loving and respecting others

That person you're making out with—yeah, that one: all actions have consequences, you know. What about his or her future? What damage will sexual activity between the two of you bring to that person's dreams, future spouse, future family, future health? If you really love that person, you won't jeopardize his or her future in any way. If you respect him or her as one of God's precious creations, you will want only what is best and right.

Loving and respecting yourself

God created you as a special, unique individual. He prepared good works in advance for you to accomplish in your life. He wants the best for you. See yourself as God sees you: a person worth waiting for, a person worth dying for, and a person worth loving forever.

Tips for staying sexually pure before marriage

- Build your relationship on friendship, not sexual intimacy.
- Enjoy activities with groups of people. The more time you spend physically alone with your boyfriend/girlfriend, the more likely you are to become sexually active.
- Hang around good friends that expect good behavior.
- Be accountable to someone besides your boyfriend/girlfriend.
- Decide to be pure. Talk about it with each other and set firm boundaries.
- Avoid alcohol and drugs. While intoxicated, you may do things you never intended, and things can happen to you that you will have no control over.
- Remember, the consequences of sex before marriage are life altering. You can always choose your conduct; you cannot choose the consequences.

Helpful resources

Sex and marriage are serious, complicated topics. Here's a list of some good books on these subjects:

- *Sex Is Not the Problem (Lust Is)* by Joshua Harris
- *I Kissed Dating Goodbye* by Joshua Harris
- *Technical Virgin: How Far is Too Far?* by Haley DiMarco
- *The Thrill of the Chaste: Finding Fulfillment While Keeping Your Clothes On* by Dawn Eden
- *Date or Soul Mate? How to Know if Someone Is Worth Pursuing in Two Dates or Less* by Neil Clark Warren
- *10 Great Dates Before You Say "I Do"* by David and Claudia Arp and Curt and Natelle Brown
- *101 Questions to Ask Before You Get Engaged* by H. Norman Wright and Gary J. Oliver
- *Saving Your Marriage Before It Starts* by Drs. Les and Leslie Parrott
- *For Women Only: What You Need to Know about the Inner Lives of Men* by Shaunti Feldhahn
- *For Men Only: A Straightforward Guide to the Inner Lives of Women* by Shaunti Feldhahn
- *Traits of a Lasting Marriage* by Jim and Sally Conway
- *The First Five Years of Marriage* by Phillip J. Swihart and Wilford Wooten
- *Love and Respect* by Dr. Emerson Eggerichs
- *Sacred Marriage* by Gary Thomas

PART 6

WHEELS

When I think about my first car, I think road trips. The summer after my husband, Kevin, and I got married, we headed west in our little Toyota station wagon. In a little over a week we visited Mount Rushmore, the Badlands, the Corn Palace, and the infamous Wall Drug store in South Dakota; saw Old Faithful spout off at Yellowstone National Park; and drove through the Teton Mountain Range.

In the United States we are blessed with both the freedom to travel and amazing places to see. Take advantage of this while you're young; don't be afraid to drive outside your comfort zone. The time will come soon enough when you'll have children, and road trips will mean answering the question "Are we there yet?" every two minutes.

To plan your road trip, visit these helpful sites:

- www.randmcnally.com/rmc/road/rtgHome.jsp
- www.roadtripamerica.com
- www.nps.gov

Chapter 25

Keys, Please

One major step in gaining independence is having your own car. More than likely, your car will be the largest purchase you'll ever make besides a house. So before heading down to your local car dealer consider:

- The average cost of owning and maintaining a $20,000 vehicle the first year is around $13,154. This cost includes monthly payments, insurance, maintenance and repairs, and Department of Motor Vehicles fees. That's almost $1,100 a month!
- Do you really need a car? If you don't need a car on a daily basis but only on the occasional

weekend, it may be cheaper to rent a car when you need one. Renting an economy car for two weekends (Friday to Sunday) per month will probably cost about $215 per month.[7] Talk about a savings!

The one sticking point is that car rental companies require renters to be at least twenty-one years old.* There are exceptions, so do some checking around.

- In most cities, mass transit is an option. The average bus or subway cost is $1.50–$2.75 per one-way trip.[8] If you used mass transit every day, you'd be looking at a cost of $120 a month. Many cities sell passes for well under $100 per month.

*Between ages twenty-one and twenty-five, expect a daily surcharge of $5 to $25. Most agencies will rent only to adults twenty-five and older.

Chapter 26

New, Used, or Leased

Okay, so you've decided that you *really* need to have a car. Should you buy new or used, or should you lease?

The cost of buying a new car

Let's look at the first-year cost of a $20,000 new car purchased with a five-year loan at 6 percent interest:

Down payment	$3,000
Monthly payment ($328.66/month)	$3,944
Insurance/maintenance/gas	$6,210[9]
Total cost for first year	$13,154

At the end of five years, considering the changing expenses, you will have spent over $53,770 to own and operate your $20,000 car.

The cost of leasing a new car

Now let's look at leasing the same car as in the example above. The lease is for five years at 6 percent interest. Here are the costs for the first year.

Down payment	$1,000
Monthly payment ($253.67/month)	$3,044
Insurance/maintenance/gas	$6,210
Total cost for first year	$10,254

However, if you look at the cost broken down over five years, you will actually spend around $47,270 leasing a vehicle—and you don't even own the car. In fact, based on a wholesale value of 39 percent, it would cost you $7,800 to purchase the vehicle you'd leased for the past five years. So to actually own and operate a $20,000 leased car for five years would cost $55,070!

The cost of buying a used car

How about buying a used car? The first-year cost of a $10,000 used car purchased with a five-year loan at 7 percent interest would be as follows:

Down payment	$2,000
Monthly payment ($158.41/month)	$1,901
Insurance/maintenance/gas	$6,201
Total cost for first year	$10,102

The total cost of owning and maintaining this used vehicle for five years runs right about $42,510.

Summing it up

At the end of five years, if you purchased a new or used car, you would have a car that you own. At the end of a car lease, you have to return the car to the dealer. In fact, when you adjust for the value of the car you now own, your five-year out-of-pocket expenses would be around $45,970 for the new car and $38,610 for the used car[10]—while you would have paid $47,270 to lease and operate a $20,000 car and, at the end of five years, have nothing to show for it.

So, is it a better deal to buy new, buy used, or lease a car? Now you can make an informed (and hopefully wise) decision.

Get some outside input

Have a parent or other family member fill in answers below.
The best car I ever owned: ______________________________
The worst car I ever owned: ______________________________
My advice on buying a car: ______________________________
____

It's a deal!

The best car deal my husband and I ever ran across was on a ten-year-old Toyota Corolla with 170,000 miles on it. We purchased this ugly beater for $1,200 with the goal of driving it for one or two years. The car lasted four years. Between the cost of the vehicle, the lower rate of insurance (we didn't carry any collision insurance due to the fact the car wasn't worth much), and minimal repairs, we probably spent only $17,000 in four years to own and operate that car.

Chapter 27

Before You Go to the Car Dealer

Figuring out what you can afford

Your total car payments, whether for one or more vehicles, should never exceed 20 percent of your take-home pay. If you're bringing home $2,000 a month, your car and auto insurance payments should be less than $400 a month.

You will want to put at least a 20 percent down payment on a car.

Your payment should be figured on a forty-eight-month loan or shorter. Paying longer on a car is not wise because if you wreck the car in year five, you will owe more than the car is worth. That means you'll have to keep making payments on a car that you can no longer drive—and that means you won't have the money to buy another vehicle.

Remember, along with the price of the car, you'll also have the expense of tax, tags, interest, vehicle registration, insurance, gasoline, and maintenance.

Sample payments

Below are sample payment amounts for variously priced cars. The figures are based on a forty-eight-month loan at 7 percent interest and a 20 percent down payment.

Cost of car	Down payment	Monthly payments
$5,000	$1,000	$95.78
$8,000	$1,600	$153.26
$10,000	$2,000	$191.57
$12,000	$2,400	$229.88
$15,000	$3,000	$287.35
$18,000	$3,600	$344.83

Now that you know how much you can afford to spend on a car, you'll need to figure out what features you really need in your car.

Required car features

1. My car needs to seat comfortably and have seat belts for
   ☐ 1 person ☐ 2 people ☐ 3–4 people
   ☐ 5 people ☐ 6 people ☐ 7 people
   ☐ 8 or more people.

IMPORTANT

Before you purchase a used car, go to www.carfax.com or www.dmv.org and get a vehicle history report. This report will inform you of any previous problems with the vehicle, such as accidents, water damage, and thefts. You will need the car's seventeen-digit VIN (Vehicle Identification Number), which is located on the dashboard and driver's side doorjamb.

2. Besides people, my car needs to be able to carry
   - ☐ nothing but little old me.
   - ☐ daily stuff for just me (briefcase, backpack, groceries).
   - ☐ suitcases for just me.
   - ☐ daily stuff for two people.
   - ☐ daily stuff for three or more people.
   - ☐ work equipment.
   - ☐ construction materials.

3. I need a car for
   - ☐ going to a grocery store and on other errands only, not driving every day.
   - ☐ short daily commutes only (less than thirty miles round-trip).
   - ☐ long daily commutes (between thirty and one hundred miles round-trip).
   - ☐ very long daily commutes (more than one hundred miles round-trip).
   - ☐ regular long business/pleasure trips (150 miles or more round-trip).
   - ☐ other ____.

4. Must-have features include

☐ 2 doors	☐ 4 doors
☐ 4x4	☐ front-wheel drive
☐ trunk	☐ flatbed
☐ air-conditioning	☐ heat
☐ Electronic Stability Control (ESC)	☐ automatic transmission
☐ stick shift	☐ front air bags

- ☐ side air bags
- ☐ cup holders
- ☐ CD player
- ☐ antilock brakes
- ☐ radio
- ☐ other ___________

Researching your car

Using your answers from questions 1–4, write a sentence that describes your ideal car: ______________________________________

____

____

____.

Now you can start researching your car. Below are some tips to get you started.

Ways to research your car

- Researching online
- Asking trusted family and friends
- Visiting car dealers to look at and test-drive cars (Shop, don't buy. Make it clear that you're researching and not purchasing. If you feel pressured to buy, leave!)
- Reading auto magazines
- Reading the auto classifieds in the newspaper

What to look for when researching cars

- Value
- Reliability
- Safety
- Fuel economy

- Operating cost
- Warranties
- Theft rates (This affects your car insurance rates)
- General features

Online car-loan calculators

- www.edmunds.com
- http://money.aol.com/calculators/autos
- www.bankrate.com

To research cars online

- www.edmunds.com
- www.consumerreports.org
- www.carsmart.com

To research auto theft rates

- www.nicb.org/cps/rde/xchg/SID-4031FE9B-2CB65AA8/nicb/hs.xsl/218.htm
- www.ncbuy.com/auto/lookup_autotheft.html
- www.auto-theft.info/Statistics.htm

To research car warranties

- www.warrantydirect.com
- www.carbuyingtips.com/warranty.htm
- www.autosite.com/content/buy/warranty/index.cfm

To check a car's safety record

- www.iihs.org
- www.nhtsa.gov/cars/testing/ncap/
- www.crashtest.com

Sticker price versus what you pay

The price on the sticker on the car window gives you an idea of what the dealership would like you to pay for the car. It is not the price you have to pay! Look up the car's real value by checking the *Kelley Blue Book* (or online at www.kbb.com), and make a reasonable offer.

Chapter 28

Car Insurance

Most states require car insurance. To find out your state regulations, go to http://info.insure.com/auto/minimum.html.

Having car insurance is more than just a requirement, it's also a good idea. Auto insurance will protect you against the cost of any damage and injury you cause to others (and possibly the cost of damage and injury to you and your vehicle) in an accident.

Types of car insurance

- *Liability coverage* is required by most states.
- *Property damage liability* covers repairing or replacing the damaged cars or properties of others.
- *Bodily injury liability* protects you from the cost of injury or death of another in an auto accident.

- *Uninsured/underinsured motorist coverage* protects you if the person at fault has no or too little insurance. Uninsured/underinsured coverage is usually only required in no-fault states. To find out if you live in a no-fault state, go to http://www.autoinsuranceindepth.com/state-minimums.html.
- *Collision, comprehensive, and medical insurance* are usually optional in most states, but it's a good idea to have them unless you can cover the cost of your car repair/replacement and medical bills in the case of an accident. *Collision coverage* pays to repair or replace your damaged car. *Comprehensive coverage* pays for nonaccident-related damage, such as fire, flood, theft, and vandalism. *Medical coverage* pays for medical expenses not covered by your health insurance or your passenger's health insurance.
- *Towing and labor coverage* pays for towing to a mechanic if your car breaks down.
- *Rental insurance* covers the cost of renting a car if your vehicle is damaged or stolen.
- *Gap coverage* covers the difference between the actual cash value of a new car and the amount left on your car loan.

Be aware that auto insurance does not cover all accident costs: you still have to pay your deductible, any costs above coverage caps, and anything excluded in your policy, such as damage done to your car because you never changed the oil.

Steps to reduce the cost of auto insurance

- Maintain a good driving record.
- If you're a student, maintain a GPA of 3.0 or higher—some insurance companies offer discounts.

- Shop around for the best deal.
- Avoid buying a car that has a high theft rate.
- Keep your car in a garage.
- Ask about discounts for antitheft devices, safety features like airbags, and low daily mileage.
- Increase your insurance deductible (just make sure you can pay it).
- Avoid add-on coverages such as car rental and towing.
- If you own a beater (car with a value of $1,000 or less), don't get collision and comprehensive coverage.
- Use one company for auto, house, renter's, and life insurance. Many insurance providers offer multipolicy discounts.

Auto-insurance comparisons

When shopping around for the best auto-insurance deals, make sure you're comparing apples with apples. Ask for the premium rates for the exact same coverage from each company.

About the car that needs coverage (fill out before you get insurance quotes)

Vehicle make and model ______________________________

Year ____________________ Mileage__________________

VIN ____________________ Amount owed ____________

Name of Lender ____________________________________

Features include (check all that apply):

☐ antilock brakes

☐ driver's side air bag

☐ passenger side air bag

- ☐ side air bags
- ☐ antitheft device (such as alarm)
- ☐ Electronic Stability Control (ESC)

Coverage needed

Research the minimum insurance required in the state where you live. You may want to purchase more insurance than your state requires. Check each type of coverage you need, and write down the amount of coverage needed.

Type of coverage	*Amount of coverage*
☐ Liability	$________________
☐ Property damage liability	$________________
☐ Bodily injury liability	$________________
☐ Uninsured/underinsured motorist	$________________
☐ Collision/comprehensive/personal injury	$________________
☐ Towing and labor	$________________
☐ Rental	$________________
☐ Gap	$________________
☐ Other	$________________

Policy comparison form

When comparing insurance companies, ask about their payment plan options. Typically, insurance premiums are billed every six months. Some companies will bill monthly, making payments easier to manage; however, a fee may be associated with using this type of plan. Download this form from http://www.simonsays.com/content/book.cfm?tab=1&pid=614860&agid=38.

Insurance company 1 ______________________________

Phone number ________________ Web site ________________

Agent's name ____

Available discounts ______________________________________

Yearly premium $ ____________ Payment plans ______________

Does the policy cover anyone who drives your car? ☐ Yes ☐ No

Insurance company 2 _____________________________________

Phone number________________Web site __________________

Agent's name ____

Available discounts ______________________________________

Yearly premium $ ____________ Payment plans ______________

Does the policy cover anyone who drives your car? ☐ Yes ☐ No

Insurance company 3 _____________________________________

Phone number________________Web site __________________

Agent's name ____

Available discounts ______________________________________

Yearly premium $ ____________ Payment plans ______________

Does the policy cover anyone who drives your car? ☐ Yes ☐ No

Chapter 29

Car Maintenance

The first step to maintaining your car is getting to know your car. Take the time to read the owner's manual and follow the manufacturer's recommended guidelines for your car's upkeep.

Routine maintenance

Task	**How often**	**Other notes**
Wash outside, vacuum inside, empty trash.	Every two weeks, or more if needed	During the winter months, if you drive over salted or treated roads, you'll need to wash the car more often.

Check tire pressure.	Once a month	Find required tire pressure for your car by looking at the sticker inside driver's doorjamb or sticker in the glove compartment.
Change oil.	Every 3,000 miles	If your car is under warranty, be sure to follow manufacturer's requirements.
Check fluids.	Every 3,000 miles	Fluids include oil, automatic transmission fluid, radiator coolant, brake fluid, and window washer fluid.
Rotate tires.	Every 6,000 miles	
Check brakes.	Every 6,000 miles	Do this at the same time you have the tires rotated.
Flush radiator.	Every 48 months	
Have routine service check.	Every 30,000 miles	Routine service checks can include a tune-up, transmission-fluid flush, check of all belts and hoses, air-filter change, and fuel-injection cleaning. Refer to your owner's manual for manufacturer's specific instructions.

Keeping a Log

Keeping a log of all maintenance performed on your car will help give it a higher resale value and maintain any warranties. Store your maintenance log in your glove compartment, along with any receipts of work done on your car. You can also track the miles per gallon (MPG) of gas your vehicle is getting. A drop in MPG often indicates something is wrong with the car.

Sample car maintenance log

Date	Odometer reading	Service or repair completed	Parts replaced or warranty work done	Where done

Sample mileage log

Date	Odometer reading	Miles trav-eled since you last filled with fuel	Gallons purchased	Miles per gallon (MPG) (miles traveled divided by gallons purchased)

Don't mess with tread

The tread on your tires is what keeps your car from slipping and sliding. Keep an eye on your tread to make sure you'll get good traction.

Routinely walk around your car and check to see if the tread on your tires is wearing evenly. If your tires are wearing unevenly, this could be an indication of under- or overinflation of tires, need for tire rotation, improper alignment, or worn shocks.

To check the tire tread, insert the edge of a penny, with Lincoln's head upside down into the grooves in the tread. If you can see the top of Lincoln's head, your tires are bald and you need new ones—like, now!

Chapter 30

Car Safety and Travel Tips

Any car can break down, so you'll want to make sure you have the following items stored in your car at all times.

- Empty fuel container
- Properly inflated spare tire and jack
- Cell phone and charger
- Flares or reflective devices
- Two flashlights—small one in the glove compartment, larger one in the trunk
- Jumper cables (Make sure you know how to use them!)
- Pocket knife
- Rope
- Basic tool kit

- First-aid kit (see Chapter 46)
- Towel
- Paper towels
- Bottled water
- Dried fruit or nuts
- Blanket
- Duct tape
- Ice scraper, gloves, tire chains, and small shovel if you live or travel in snowy/icy areas

Tips for safe driving

- Make sure everyone in car is wearing a seat belt.
- Don't drink and drive.
- Don't drive tired.
- Be patient and courteous.
- Do not make eye contact with other drivers.
- Keep your doors locked and windows up.
- Keep plenty of space between you and the car in front of you.
- Avoid conflict.
- Give yourself extra travel time.
- Take a defensive driving course.
- Don't leave the car running in a garage.
- Don't leave children or animals in the car.

Travel tips

- Know your route. You can easily find directions online at www.mapquest.com, http://maps.yahoo.com, or http://maps.google.com.
- Bring the phone number of your destination with you.
- Check road, traffic, and construction conditions before you leave. Call 511, or go online to www.fhwa.dot.gov/trafficinfo, or www.traffic.com. Maps on Yahoo or Google also have traffic update features.
- If you need to ask for directions, ask a store clerk, a family, or a woman with children.
- Use valet parking when you can.
- Carry just one credit card, and don't carry all your cash in your wallet.
- Use your work address on luggage instead of your home address.
- Park in well-lighted lots as close to an entrance as possible.
- Lock car doors every time you get out of your vehicle, even at a gas station.
- If attacked, scream LOUDLY and RUN!

PART 7
GOTTA EAT

Eating a constant diet of ramen noodles can get boring, not to mention that it's deprived of almost any nutritional value.

Learning to cook is not only an essential survival skill; it's also a great way to entertain and impress the opposite sex.

The next few chapters will cover everything you need to get started in the kitchen.

Chapter 31

Kitchen Basics—What You Need to Get Started

The really basic basics

1-quart saucepan with lid
3-quart saucepan with lid
8-quart stockpot
7-inch nonstick skillet with lid
10-inch nonstick skillet with lid
13x9-inch glass baking dish
8-inch square baking dish
2-quart casserole with lid
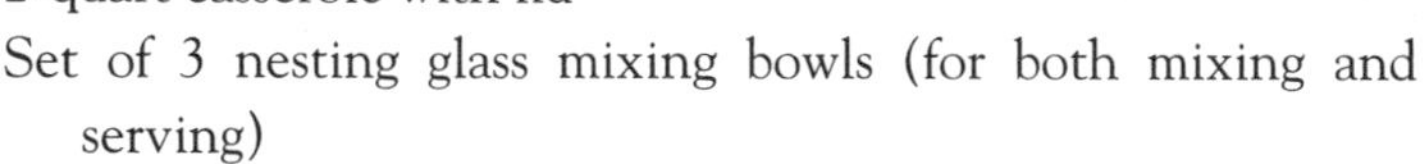
Set of 3 nesting glass mixing bowls (for both mixing and serving)
1 set of measuring spoons
1 set of measuring cups

2-cup glass liquid measuring cup
1 or 2 cookie sheets
Cooling rack
Colander

Essential kitchen tools

Vegetable peeler
1 rubber spatula
Paring knife
Large slicing knife
Cutting board
Can opener
Ladle
Pot holders, at least 2
Vegetable scrub brush
Plastic wrap
Sealable plastic food storage bags
Scrubbing pad
2 wooden spoons
Large chopping knife
Whisk
Tongs
Timer
Pasta server
Kitchen towels
Dish drainer
Aluminum foil
Trivet
2 food turners, one rubber and one metal
Permanent marker

Essential small appliances

Coffeemaker
Toaster (the kind that toasts both bread and bagels)
Microwave
Blender

Just beyond the basics

For those of you who are a little more ambitious in the kitchen, here are some other items you may need:

A note on small appliances

We have all purchased some kitchen gadget or small appliance that we used once or twice before it made its way to the dark corner of a pantry or basement. Before you buy the latest "must have" kitchen item, ask yourself:

- Do I already own a kitchen tool or appliance that can do the exact same thing?
- How often will I *really* use it?
- Do I have a place to store it?

For cooking

6-quart Dutch oven
2 round cake pans
Metal roasting pan with lid
Pie plate, glass
Teakettle
Vegetable steamer
Loaf pan, 1 or 2
Muffin pan (for 12 muffins)
Pizza pan

More kitchen tools

Rolling pin
Grater
Pastry blender
Meat fork
Citrus juicer
Instant cooking thermometer
Garlic press
Potato masher
Kitchen scissors
Set of good knives
Minichopper
Pastry brush

More small appliances

Waffle iron
Electric mixer
Crock-Pot/slow cooker
Rice cooker
Coffee grinder

Other nice-to-have items

Outdoor grill (gas or charcoal)
Electric popcorn popper

Shopping for kitchen items

Shopping at thrift stores, such as Goodwill, for all your kitchen items will save you tons of money. Plus, if marriage is somewhere on the horizon, there's no need to buy new stuff now. You'll get plenty in the way of shower and/or wedding gifts.

Appliance advice

(To be filled out by a family member or friend)

A small appliance I bought and never used more than a couple of times was ____

____.

A small appliance I can't live without is ____________________.

Chapter 32

A Well-Stocked Pantry and Fridge

Before you start cooking, you'll want to have some basic food items on hand. These items fall into three categories: things that need to be stored in the refrigerator, things that don't (pantry items), and seasonings (herbs and spices, etc.). All food items need to be stored in well-sealed containers.

Essential refrigerated items

- Ketchup
- Mayonnaise
- Parmesan cheese
- Eggs
- Worcestershire sauce
- Pancake syrup
- Mustard
- Butter
- Fruit juice
- Milk
- Pickles
- Hot sauce

Balsamic vinegar
Fruit jam or jelly
Cheese (grated for easy cooking, sliced for sandwiches)
Salsa
Soy sauce

Essential pantry items

Flour, all-purpose or whole-wheat
Granulated sugar
Brown sugar
Olive oil
Baking soda
Egg noodles
Peanut butter
Pasta sauce
Biscuit Mix
Chicken and beef bouillon
Pasta—spaghetti, penne, angel hair, macaroni
Vegetable oil
Nonstick cooking spray
Baking powder
Rice
Breakfast cereal
Tuna
Vinegar, white or cider
Pancake Syrup
Shortening (such as Crisco)

Essential seasonings

Salt
Chili powder
Oregano
Italian seasoning
Pepper
Basil
Nutmeg
Ginger
Vanilla extract
Cinnamon
Sage
Cumin

How long do spices last on the shelf?

For years (more like a decade) I had a can of poultry spice that my mother gave me. I used it every once in a great while, but I never knew when to throw it away.

Spices and herbs don't go bad if stored properly, but they do lose their intensity. The trick to preserving spices and herbs for as long as possible is storing them in well-sealed containers.

Don't store herbs and spices over the stove, in high humidity, or in freezer or refrigerator.

Another tip:

Don't shake your spices and herbs out over the food you're cooking. The steam rising from the cooking food can enter the seasoning container and spoil the contents.

How long do condiments last?

Always check the manufacturer's expiration date on the label. However, here are some general guidelines for condiments and other refrigerated items once they're opened and stored in the refrigerator.

Item	Duration
Sour cream	2 weeks
Salsa, eggs	1 month
Salad dressing, butter	3 months
Ketchup, jams, and jellies	6 months
Soy sauce, mustard, hot sauce, pancake syrup	1 year
Worcestershire sauce	2 years
Vinegar	4 years

Chapter 33

Food, Glorious Food

Food fuels our bodies. Food also often serves as a comforter, a reward, or social icebreaker. The wrong food, too much (or too little) food, or spoiled food can make us sick or even kill us.

Do you know enough about food to make good decisions about what you eat? What size is a serving, really? Is it safe to eat that week-old pizza in the fridge? Are there food pyramids in Egypt?

Why does what you eat matter? Because the results of not eating properly are devastating and life-shortening.

Poor eating habits can lead to . . .

- Heart disease
- Diabetes
- Cancer
- High blood pressure
- Fatigue
- Stroke

- Obesity
- Decrease in your ability to learn, focus, and concentrate
- Suppressed immune system, so your body gets sick more often and you stay sick for a longer period of time

For pregnant women, poor nutrition can lead to . . .

- Stillbirths
- Toxemia
- Birth defects
- Other major health complications for both mother and child
- Anemia
- Low birth weight
- Poor fetal development

Note: Pregnant women have higher and different nutritional needs than listed below. If you are pregnant, think you are pregnant, or thinking about becoming pregnant, consult with your doctor regarding your dietary needs.

What does your body really need?

According to the United States Department of Agriculture (USDA), most of us need the following foods daily:

6 ounces of grains, with at least 3.4 ounces being whole grains
2.6 cups of vegetables
2.1 cups of fruit
3.1 cups of milk
5.6 ounces of meat and beans
7.2 teaspoons of oils

The USDA breaks down your vegetable requirements even further, stating that every week you should eat the following:

3.3 cups of dark green vegetables
2.3 cups of orange vegetables
3.0 cups of beans
3.4 cups of starchy vegetables
6.6 cups of other vegetables

Know your veggies

Dark green vegetables include

Bok choy
Broccoli
Collard greens
Dark green leafy lettuce (not your typical head of iceberg lettuce)
Kale
Mustard greens
Romaine lettuce
Spinach
Watercress

Orange vegetables include

Acorn squash
Butternut squash
Carrots
Hubbard squash
Pumpkins
Sweet potatoes/yams

Dry beans and peas include

Black beans
Kidney beans
Garbanzo beans (chickpeas)
Lentils
Lima beans
Navy beans
Pinto beans
Soybeans

Split peas
White beans
Tofu

Starchy vegetables include

Corn
Green peas
Lima beans
Potatoes

Other vegetables include

Artichokes
Asparagus
Bean sprouts
Beets
Brussels sprouts
Cabbage
Celery
Cucumbers
Eggplants
Green beans
Green or red peppers
Iceberg (head) lettuce
Mushrooms
Okra
Onions
Parsnips
Tomatoes
Tomato juice
Turnips
Wax beans
Zucchini

Fruit

Unless you plan to cut up all the fruit you eat, measuring how many cups a banana, apple, or pear will fill is a tad tricky. So here's a handy list to help you figure how much fruit you need to eat to get in your 2.1 cups per day. Each item below is roughly equal to one cup.

1 small apple
1 large banana

1 medium grapefruit
1 large orange
1 medium pear
1 small wedge of watermelon
2–3 medium plums
8 large strawberries
2 medium wedges of cantaloupe
32 grapes

Eating a rainbow

The color of fruits and vegetables actually indicates the various nutrients they contain. To ensure that you get a well-balanced diet, try eating fruits and vegetables from every color of the rainbow each week.

Red	Tomatoes, pink grapefruit, strawberries, raspberries, cherries, watermelon, red peppers, beets, red apples, cranberries
Orange	Oranges (duh!), pumpkins, carrots, mangoes, sweet potatoes, cantaloupes, tangerines, peaches, papayas, nectarines
Yellow	Lemons, yellow squashes, pineapples, wax beans, corn, yellow apples, bananas
Green	Spinach, green peas, green beans, avocados, broccoli, cabbage, bok choy, kiwi, lettuce
Blue	Blueberries, blackberries
Purple	Grapes, eggplants, prunes, plums, purple cabbage

White (Yes, I know white is not a color in the rainbow. Just humor me.)	Onions, garlic, celery, pears, leeks, scallions, cauliflower, navy beans, white beans, potatoes

Going with the grain

The grains food group consists of foods made primarily with ingredients like wheat, rice, corn, and oats. Grains generally fall into one of two categories: refined and whole grain.

Refined grain goes through a process that removes the bran and germ, thus removing dietary fiber, iron, and many B vitamins. Refined grains may be enriched, which means that some B vitamins and iron have been added back in. However, the fiber is not.

Whole-grain products use the entire grain (hence the name). Therefore, whole-grain foods are a good source of fiber, iron, and B vitamins.

Refined-grain products include

- White flour
- White bread
- Grits
- Corn tortillas
- Crackers made with white flour
- Pretzels made with refined grain
- Degermed cornmeal
- Regular (not whole-wheat) pasta—spaghetti, macaroni, noodles, etc.
- Breakfast cereals made with refined wheat, corn, or rice
- White rice

Whole-grain foods include

Whole-wheat flour
Popcorn
Whole-wheat cereal flakes
Whole-wheat bread
Bulgur
Wild rice
Brown rice
Oatmeal
Whole-wheat pasta
Whole-grain cornmeal
Whole-wheat tortillas

What does an ounce of grain look like?

Remember: you need 6 ounces of grains daily, with at least 3.4 ounces being from whole grain.

Product	1-ounce portion	Typical serving portions
Bagel	1 mini bagel	1 large bagel = 4 oz.
Biscuits	1 small (2-inch) biscuit	1 large biscuit = 2 oz.
Breads	1 regular slice	2 regular slices = 2 oz.
Crackers	5 whole-wheat crackers	7 square or round refined-grain crackers
English muffin	1/2 muffin	1 muffin = 2 oz.
Muffins	1 mini muffin	1 large muffin = 3 oz.
Oatmeal	1/2 cup cooked	1 packet of instant = 1 oz
Pancakes	1 pancake	3 pancakes = 3 oz.
Popcorn	3 cups, popped	1 microwave bag = 4 oz.
Ready-to-eat breakfast cereal	1 cup flakes	

Rice	½ cup cooked	1 cup cooked = 2 oz.
Pasta (regular, not whole-grain)	½ cup cooked	1 cup cooked = 2 oz.
Tortillas	1 6-inch tortilla	1 12-inch tortilla = 4 oz.

Got milk?

Dairy products give us calcium and vitamin D, nutrients needed for strong bones. Between the ages of nineteen and fifty, you need 1,200 mg of calcium and 400 IU of vitamin D daily. Eating or drinking 3.1 cups of diary products typically supplies the calcium and vitamin D you need.

Dairy product	**Calcium (mg)**	**Vitamin D (IU)**
1 cup milk, skim or low-fat	301	98
1 cup low-fat yogurt	350	100
2 oz. cheddar cheese	236	Trace
1 cup low-fa t cottage cheese	138	40
1/2 cup low-fat ice cream	91.7	Trace

Meat, beans, and so much more

Besides meat and beans, poultry, fish, eggs, nuts, and seeds are included in the "meat and beans" food group. These foods contain high quantities of protein needed for healthy bones, muscles, cartilage, skin, and blood. They're often a good source of B and E vitamins, iron, magnesium, and zinc.

The key to making good choices in the meat and beans category is to think lean and varied. Lean choices will keep your fat intake down. Varying your selection ensures that you get the unique nutrients available in the different options.

Meats include

Beef
Pork
Veal
Ham
Lamb
Venison

Poultry includes

Chicken
Duck
Turkey

Eggs include

Um . . . chicken eggs (other eggs count, but try finding them in a grocery store!)

Fish includes

Catfish
Flounder
Tuna
Shellfish, such as crab, clams, lobster, and shrimp
Cod
Salmon
Trout

Nuts and seeds include

Almonds
Peanut butter
Cashews
Peanuts

Pecans
Pumpkin seeds
Sunflower seeds
Sesame seeds

Dry beans and peas include

Black beans
Kidney beans
Lentils
Navy beans
Soybeans
Tofu
Split peas
Veggie or garden burgers

What does 1 ounce of meat, beans, etc., look like?

Remember: you need 5.6 ounces of foods from this category daily.

Food	**1-ounce portion**	**Typical serving portions**
Beef	1 oz. cooked lean beef	1 small steak = 4 oz. 1 small hamburger = 3 oz.
Pork	1 oz. lean pork or ham	1 small pork chop = 3 oz.
Chicken	1 oz. cooked chicken or turkey without skin	1 small chicken breast half = 3oz.
Fish	1 oz. cooked fish or shellfish	1 can tuna, drained = 3 oz. 1 salmon steak = 5 oz.
Eggs	1 egg	
Nuts	12 almonds, 24 pistachios 1 tablespoon peanut butter	1 oz. nuts = 2 oz. when counting ounces in this food group

Seeds	½ oz. of pumpkin or sunflower seeds	1 oz. seeds = 2 oz. when counting ounces in this food group
Dry beans and peas	½ cup cooked black beans ½ cup refried beans ½ cup split peas	1 cup bean soup = 2 oz. 1 cup split pea soup = 2 oz.
Soybeans	½ cup tofu ½ cup roasted soybeans	1 soy burger = 2 oz.

Hey, I thought you said beans and peas were vegetables!

They are. However, because of the high amount of protein in dried beans and peas, they're also included in the same group as meat. If you eat a fair amount of meat each week, than count the beans you eat as veggies. If you shy away from meat products, count the dry beans and peas you eat in the "meat and beans" group.

Oils

Oils are fats that are liquid at room temperature. Since most of us get more than the daily requirement of oil in our regular diet, making sure you get 7.2 teaspoons of oil a day usually isn't a problem. But you do need to know the difference between oils and solid fats.

Oils from plants or nuts do not contain cholesterol. The polyunsaturated and monounsaturated fats in oils give you energy, provide essential fatty acids, and help with the absorption of fat-soluble vitamins.

Oils or foods rich in oils include

Canola oil
Olive oil
Sunflower oil
Olives
Mayonnaise
Corn oil
Soybean oil
Nuts
Avocados
Peanut butter

Solid fats

Solid fats are fats that are solid at room temperature. Most solid fats come from animal fat or can be made from vegetable oils through hydrogenation. Solid fats are high in saturated fat and contain trans fat, which can raise blood cholesterol levels.

Saturated fats should take up less than 10 percent of your total calories in a day. If you need 2,000 calories per day, less than 200 calories should come from saturated fats. That's not much when you consider that one tablespoon of butter contains 100 saturated-fat calories, one cup of chocolate ice cream has 125 saturated fat calories, and a three-ounce hamburger contains 120.

Solid fats or foods rich in solid fats include

Butter
Stick margarine
Shortening
Half-and-half
Ice cream
Croissant
Pound cake
Coconut or palm-kernel oil
Beef, pork, and chicken fat
Heavy cream
Sour cream
Bacon
Pork sausage
Icing

The other food group

Look over the last few pages, and you won't find gravy, french fries, or candy bars listed in any of the food groups. These fall in another group normally referred to as "junk food." Junk foods are defined by their high amount of fats and/or sugars and lack of nutritional value.

Now, the occasional Snickers or Big Mac is not going to kill you. But a steady diet of junk food could lead to your demise for two reasons:

1. The ingredients in junk food, like saturated fats and lots of added sugar, can cause heart disease, diabetes, cancer, and other nasty diseases.
2. The fat and sugar in junk food means more calories. One hundred extra calories a day equals a ten-pound weight gain per year. Twelve ounces of soda has about 155 calories; two chocolate-covered peanut-butter cups have 232 calories; and one medium order of french fries has about 460 calories. You do the math.

Since we often eat junk food instead of something more nutritious, like a doughnut instead of a bowl of whole-grain cereal, our bodies don't get the nutrition they need. A lack of good nutrition leads to the systems in our bodies breaking down, making it much easier for us to get sick.

What do you do?

When it comes to food, put your time, energy, and money into eating what you need in each food group. If you really eat 2.6 cups of vegetables a day, 2.1 cups of fruit, 3.4 ounces of whole grains, and so on, you'll find that you really aren't hungry for the junk food you don't need.

To find out exactly what food your body requires, visit www.mypyramid.gov, click on "My Pyramid Plan," fill in your personal information, and get a customized food plan.

Other sources of vitamin D and calcium

Vitamin D

- Sunshine—15 minutes for light-skinned people, or 3 hours for dark-skinned people, will supply enough vitamin D for a few days
- 3 oz. of salmon contains 530 IU
- 3 oz. of tuna contains 200 IU
- 1 egg yolk contains 20 IU

Calcium

- 3 oz. of salmon contains 208 mg
- ½ cup cooked spinach contains 120 mg
- 1 cup broccoli contains 90 mg
- 1 oz. cooked dried white beans contains 160 mg
- 1 oz dry roasted almonds contains 80 mg

Beans, the powerful fruit

Beans are . . .

- cheap.
- high in fiber. One serving of beans contains 20 percent or more of your required daily fiber.
- equivalent to meat as a protein source.
- packed with the vitamins and minerals of a vegetable.
- low in fat.

How to tell if food is really whole-grain

1. Look at the color.

Brown color does not guarantee that a bread, pasta, or rice is made with whole grain. However, if you're looking at white rice, bread, or pasta, you can be fairly certain they contain refined grains.

2. Read the label.

Ignore blurbs like "made with," "100 percent wheat", "good source" or "whole grain" on the product packaging. Instead, read the ingredient list. One of the first ingredients should start with the word "whole" or "oat." Products with the black and gold "Whole Grain" stamp of the Whole Grains Council are guaranteed to have at least half a serving of whole grains per serving of the product.

Note: oats and popcorn are always whole grains.

Chapter 34

Menu Planning

Before you go to the grocery store, know what you need to buy. The only way to do that, of course, is to plan out your meals for the next week or two. Menu planning saves you money, time, and stress.

- *Money*—Having meals planned out will allow you to buy only what you need, limiting impulse shopping. It also will eliminate extra trips to the grocery store (where you always ending up spending more than you intended) and unplanned dinners out (another budget buster). You'll also waste less food.
- *Time*—Knowing ahead of time what you plan to purchase will save you tons of time in the store. Planning

eliminates those extra runs to the grocery store, another time saver.

- *Stress*—Planning eliminates the daily worry about what you're going to eat and the stress of going to the store and trying to remember what you need to purchase, as well as the frustration of coming home and realizing you forgot to buy a key ingredient for a meal you're preparing.

How to plan a menu

Step 1 Decide whether you want to and have the time for grocery shopping once a week or once every two weeks.

Step 2 Look at your schedule and determine how many meals you will be eating at home during that time period.

Step 3 Create a planning calendar and note the meals you won't need to prepare at home.

Step 4 Check grocery ads in the newspaper or online for the sales that week. You're looking for the best prices on meats, fruits, vegetables, and diary products. Write down sale items that appeal to you.

Step 5 List some meals you could make with those sale items. Example: Lean ground beef is on sale. With ground beef, you could make tacos, chili, meat loaf, or hamburgers. Or, say, fresh spinach is on sale. With spinach you could make a salad or a quiche.

Step 6 Decide what meals you want to make and start filling in the planning calendar. As you're planning meals, think variety—and make sure you're meeting your daily nutritional needs. How much time you have to prepare meals will factor into what recipes you choose. Plan for breakfast, lunch, and dinner—and don't forget snacks.

Step 7 Look at the recipes you've chosen for the week, and list all ingredients needed that you do not have on hand. Include in that list any other items, like fruit, vegetables, and breakfast items, from your menu plan that you need to purchase.

Step 8 Go grocery shopping!

Making meals with friends— a fun way to plan meals

Once a month, invite friends or roommates (two to four people) to spend part of one day cooking with you. Before you meet, have everyone select an ingredient from the meat-and-beans food group (beef, poultry, eggs, fish, or dried beans). You'll want to find out if anyone has dietary restrictions or food allergies so everyone can work around them.

Each person selects a main dish (that will serve at least six adults) that he or she would like to make using the main ingredient they chose and purchases all items needed to prepare the recipe. Also, have everyone bring some quart-size freezer bags and plastic freezer containers.

Gather together and spend the next few hours cooking. Let food cool a little, then divide it up in equal portions among you and put in appropriate freezer containers. Each person then takes home a portion of each dish. Immediately refrigerate food you will eat within the next forty-eight hours, and freeze the rest. Ta-da! You have dinners for at least the next week or two.

Some good freezer meals

- Soups, chili, or stews
- Casseroles
- Pot pies
- Meat loaf
- Lasagna
- Taco meat

Sample planning calendar

	Sunday	Monday	Tuesday	Wednesday	Thursday	Friday	Saturday
Breakfast			Meeting Scott for breakfast				
Lunch	Eating with friends after church			Going to lunch with coworkers			
Dinner						Watching game at Johnsons'	Going out
Snack							

Sample calendar with menu plan

	Sunday	Monday	Tuesday	Wednesday	Thursday	Friday	Saturday
Breakfast	Cold cereal, pear Hot tea	Oatmeal Blueberries Orange juice	Meeting Scott for breakfast	Cold cereal Orange Hot coffee	Oatmeal Banana Orange juice	Cold cereal Pineapple Hot tea	Scrambled eggs Whole-wheat toast Orange juice
Lunch	Eating with friends after church	Leftover chili Salad Cottage cheese	Chicken salad made with leftover grilled chicken Pineapple Yogurt	Going to lunch with coworkers	Chicken salad Whole-grain crackers Kiwi Yogurt	Tuna-salad sandwich on whole-wheat bread Carrot sticks Blueberries	Leftover lasagna Carrot sticks
Dinner	Chili Grated cheese Salad Whole-wheat roll Milk	Grilled chicken breast Wild rice Broccoli	Leftover chili Salad Baked potato Milk	Having friends over Lasagna Salad Whole-wheat rolls Apple crisp	Leftover lasagna Salad Roll	Watching game at Johnsons'—bring chips and dip	Going out
Snack	Popcorn	Carrot sticks with dip	Banana	Popcorn	Broccoli with dip		Popcorn

While cooking, provide your guests with healthy snacks or sandwiches. Snacking on the food you're cooking is a sure way to pass around germs and bacteria. Plus, having snack food along with some background music and good conversation turns this event from plain cooking to a cooking party!

How to plan menus when someone else is cooking for you

For your first few years away from home, you may be getting all your meals from a school cafeteria, or you may live in a Greek house that has a cook. In these circumstances you may not have a choice of what food is served, but you always have a choice of what you actually eat. A few helpful hints:

- Keep portions small.
- Drink water, milk, or unsweetened tea during meals.
- Avoid getting in a rut and eating the same thing every day.
- When you eat out, order something you don't normally get in your cafeteria or house.
- Don't be afraid to suggest items you would like to see on the menu.
- Eat raw: raw vegetables, fresh fruit, dark-green leafy salads.

Menu-planning tips

- Try to use an ingredient in more than one recipe. Example: Use ground beef to make chili and spaghetti sauce. Or roast a chicken and use leftovers to make soup or a casserole.
- If you make a big meal, plan on eating it for the next couple of days, or put some in the freezer for the following week. Just remember it's still there!
- Once every two weeks, try a new recipe.

Chapter 35

Going to the Grocery Store—Without Your Mother

You've planned your meals and made a list of the food you need to purchase. You'll want to add any needed household items to that list, such as toothpaste and laundry detergent. Now you're off to the grocery store. What do you need to know to make the best purchases and get the most for your money?

Eat before you shop

Going to the grocery store hungry causes one of two reactions: either you'll buy everything in sight because you're starving, or you'll buy very little because you're so hungry you can't decide what to purchase. So eat a little something before you go shopping.

The lay of the land

The layout of grocery stores is designed to make you purchase more items, especially foods with a higher profit margin for the store. You'll find produce, dairy, bread, and meat products along the outside walls, with the most commonly purchased items in the back corner. To get to these items, you have to walk by all the processed foods located on the interior aisles. At the ends of the aisles, or even in the middle, displays are set up to tempt you to buy items not on your list.

Being aware of your grocery store's layout will not only help you get your shopping done quicker but also will keep you from buying impulsively. Grocery store managers know this, which is why every so often, stores rearrange where food is shelved.

Your best bet is to shop the perimeter of the store and to keep to your list.

Shopping for produce (fruits and vegetables)

- Buy what's in season to get the best price and highest quality.
- Don't buy anything that is overripe, bruised, discolored, mildewed, or mushy.
- Don't buy more than you'll eat.

Selecting fruit

Apples—harvested in late summer through fall. Apples store well, so they're available year-round. Apples should be firm, crisp, and have good color. Eating varieties include Red Delicious, Golden Delicious, Gala, and Fuji. Baking varieties include Rome Beauty, Winesap, and Granny Smith.

Apricots—fresh in June and July. Apricots should be plump, juicy, and have an all-over orange color.

Bananas—imported and available year-round. Buy yellow bananas if you plan to eat them in the next few days; otherwise purchase bananas with green tips and let them ripen at home. Lots of small black spots on the banana indicate it's overripe. Large black spots show up when the banana is bruised.

Blueberries—freshest May through August. Look for blueberries that are plump and have a uniform dark blue color.

Cherries—freshest May through August. Look for bright, glossy, plump cherries with dark color, if a red variety—or a straw color if you're purchasing Rainer cherries. Avoid cherries that are shriveled or have dark purple bruises.

Grapefruit—freshest January through May. Pick out firm, heavy fruit. Avoid grapefruit with skin that is rough, wrinkled, or soft.

Grapes—available year-round. Grapes should be firmly attached to the stem and have a good, consistent color. Don't buy dry wrinkled grapes, unless you're buying a box of raisins.

Kiwi fruit—available year-round. Kiwi is ripe when its skin gives a little under light pressure, but you can still buy firm kiwi—they will ripen in a few days if kept at room temperature. Avoid soft, shriveled, or moldy kiwi.

Lemons and limes—available year-round. Look for fruit that has bright, rich, even color. Avoid limes and lemons with dull color or decay.

Cantaloupe—freshest May through September. Ripe cantaloupe has a yellowish cast to its rind and smells like cantaloupe.

After purchasing cantaloupe, set it out at room temperature for a couple of days before eating. Don't buy cantaloupe that is soft or moldy.

Honeydew—available year-round, but most abundant July through October. Pick up the melon and press gently on the end opposite the stem. If the end is soft and the melon smells fruity, it's ripe. Avoid white or hard-skinned honeydew.

Watermelon—available May through September. A ripe watermelon has a slightly dull-colored rind and is well-rounded. The inside flesh should have no white streaks but be a nice shade of red.

Nectarines—available June through September. Look for plump and rich-colored fruits that are slightly soft. Bright fruit that is firm will ripen in a few days at room temperature. Don't buy nectarines that are hard or shriveled.

Oranges—available year round. A good orange is firm and heavy, with a brightly colored peel. Avoid oranges that feel light or have a very rough peel.

Peaches—available May through November. Buy peaches that are firm or a little soft, with red-and-yellow skin. Avoid hard peaches with any green coloring. Peaches bruise easily, so don't purchase fruit that is bruised or has dark spots.

Pears—freshest August through May, depending on variety. The color of pears differ, but their skin should be firm or a little soft. Ripen at home for a few days at room temperature before eating. Avoid shriveled or very hard pears.

Pineapples—freshest March through June. Pineapples should have a bright golden yellow color and smell like pineapple.

Don't buy pineapples that are a dull yellowish-green color, are dried out, or have sunken points.

Strawberries—harvested as early as January, but most abundant May through June. Look for berries that are bright red and have the cap stem still attached. Avoid berries that are light-colored or moldy.

Selecting vegetables

Artichokes—available April through June. Artichokes should be plump, heavy, and compact. Avoid artichokes that are starting to open up or have large brown spots.

Asparagus—most available in the spring. Spears should be round and smooth, have compact tips, and be a rich green color. Don't buy asparagus with decaying tips or ridged spears.

Green beans—available year-round. Look for fresh, bright, tender beans. Avoid beans that are large, bumpy, thick, or wilted.

Broccoli—available year-round. Broccoli should have firm, compact heads with no flowers opened. Don't buy bröccoli that has enlarged or open buds or any yellow coloring.

Cabbage—available year-round. Cabbage heads should be firm and heavy, with fresh-looking outer leaves. Wilted, decayed, or yellow outer leaves indicate a bad cabbage.

Carrots—available year-round. A good carrot is evenly formed, has good color, and is firm. Avoid carrots that are greenish at the top.

Cauliflower—freshest September through January. White, compact, solid, and clean cauliflower is what you want to buy. Avoid cauliflower with any discoloration.

Celery—available year-round. Stalks should be solid, with fresh leaves on top. Avoid wilted, limp celery.

Corn—freshest May through September. Look for corn with fresh husks, green silk, and plump but not too mature kernels. Don't buy wormy, underdeveloped or overdeveloped corn.

Cucumbers—best supply in summer. Cucumbers should be green all over, firm, and not too large. Avoid yellowing or oversized cucumbers.

Eggplant—most abundant in late summer. Look for bright, shiny, uniform color. You want an eggplant that is firm and heavy. Soft, shriveled, dull-colored eggplants aren't worth your dime.

Lettuce—available year-round. Any variety of lettuce should be crisp and have good color. Don't buy wilted, brown, or mushy lettuce.

Mushrooms—available year-round. Mushrooms should be firm, evenly colored white or brown (depending on variety), and the cap should be closed around the stem. If the top of the mushroom has opened and you can see dark brown under the cap, don't buy it.

Onions—available year-round. Onions should be hard and dry with small necks. Avoid onions that are mushy or have very soft necks.

Peppers—most plentiful in late summer. Look for peppers that have a deep, glossy color on the outside. You want them to be firm and heavy. Wilted or soft peppers are nasty.

Potatoes—available year-round. Whether you're buying a new potato, baking potato, or sweet potato, you want it to be firm and free of blemishes. Don't buy green or shriveled potatoes.

Summer squash (this includes zucchini, crookneck, and pattypan)—freshest in summertime. Look for squash that is glossy and firm. Avoid dull, hard, oversized squash.

Tomatoes—freshest in summertime. Tomatoes should be smooth, with a rich color, and slightly soft. Avoid soft, bruised, and cracked tomatoes.

Shopping in the meat department

In a grocery store's meat department, you'll find chicken, turkey, lamb, fish, and shellfish, as well as beef and pork.

All meat in the United States is inspected by the United States Department of Agriculture (USDA) and graded according to quality. There's a big difference in taste and tenderness between the top and bottom grade, so it's important to know what you're buying.

Beef grades

USDA Prime—the highest grade, given to beef that is tender, juicy, and has lots of marbling. (Marbling is the fat within the flesh of the meat.)

USDA Choice—high-quality meat with less marbling than Prime.

USDA Select—leaner but less flavorful than Choice or Prime meats. Select meat tends to be a little tough and often needs to be marinated before cooking.

Lamb grades

USDA Prime—highest quality lamb. It's tender, juicy, and flavorful.

USDA Choice—high-quality lamb with less marbling than Prime.

Note: Meat from older sheep is called mutton.

Pork grades

USDA Acceptable—the only grade you will find in stores.

USDA Utility—not sold in grocery stores.

Poultry grades

Poultry includes chicken, turkey, duck, goose, guinea, and pigeon.

Grade A—the only grade you want to buy for ready-to-cook poultry. Grade A poultry is meaty, well developed, and free of broken bones and pinfeathers.

Reduced priced meat and poultry

When meat or poultry reaches its "Sell by" date, grocery stores often reduce the price 40 to 60 percent. These meats are safe to buy; however, plan on cooking them within twenty-four hours after purchase, or put them in the freezer immediately.

How to buy fish and other seafood

- Buy from a reputable and clean store.
- Fish should be refrigerated or on ice.
- If it smells like fish, don't buy it.

- Fish's eyes should be clear, not cloudy.
- Fish should have firm and shiny meat.
- If fish meat is darkening or drying, don't buy it.
- Only buy live lobsters or crabs that move their legs.
- Tap live clams, oysters, and mussels. If they don't close up, don't buy them.
- Shrimp should have firm, white meat and smell like saltwater.

Other shopping tips

- Grocers reduce the price of day-old bread and baked goods. These usually are on a separate rack in the bakery section.
- Frozen fruit can be cheaper than fresh fruit, plus you can thaw only the amount you need.
- Frozen orange-juice concentrate is cheaper than refrigerated orange juice.
- To avoid spoilage, go home directly after grocery shopping and put away refrigerated and frozen items immediately.

When you get home from the grocery store

- Put frozen items in freezer.
- Put chilled or refrigerated items in fridge.
- Divide up meat. Put what you're going to cook in the next two days in the refrigerator. Freeze the rest.
- Place bananas and unripe fruit in a bowl on counter or table. Put fully ripened fruits and vegetables in refrigerator.
- Put everything else away.

To save time

When you bring ground beef home from the grocery store, brown it with some chopped onions and garlic. Let beef cool a little, then divide and place in freezer bags. Freeze until you need it for spaghetti sauce, chili, or any other dish that calls for ground beef. You can also roast chicken, chop up the meat, and freeze it to use in soups and casseroles.

Storing meat and poultry

Type of food	**How long you can store in the refrigerator**	**How long you can store in the freezer**
Beef roasts and steaks	3–5 days	6 months
Ground beef	1–2 days	3 months
Lamb	3–5 days	6 months
Pork roasts and chops	3–5 days	4 months
Pork sausage	1–2 days	1 month
Whole chicken or turkey (fresh)	1–2 days	1 year
Chicken or turkey pieces (fresh)	1–2 days	9 months
Fish and shellfish (fresh)	1 day	2 months
Sliced deli meat	3–5 days	1–2 months
Hot dogs	Opened—7 days Unopened—2 weeks	1–2 months

Freezing any type of meat or poultry

- If meat was packaged in the store and covered with plastic wrap, remove packaging.
- Meat packaged by the manufacturer (such as whole turkeys or hot dogs) can be kept in original packaging.
- Wrap meat tightly in freezer paper or place in smallest-size freezer bag it can fit in. Squeeze out as much air as possible, and seal securely.
- Place meat in a second freezer bag. Again, squeeze out air and seal securely.
- Write the meat type and the date purchased on the package.
- Place in freezer.

Note: If you're planning to buy meat in bulk, you may want to invest in a vacuum-sealing device. Put meat in the manufacture's specified bag, and the vacuum sealer will remove all the air and seal the meat tightly. This process allows you to store meat in the freezer for longer periods of time.

Food and roomies

If there are some foods you just don't want to share with your roommate, simply write your initials on the package using a permanent marker when you take it out of the grocery bag at home.

Chapter 36

Good to Eat and Easy to Cook

You need to eat, and you want to eat well. But few of us have hours to spend in the kitchen. In this chapter you'll find some quick-fix or multiuse recipes. Don't be afraid to modify recipes to your own taste. If you know you don't like garlic, don't add it. If you think adding olives would make the recipe better, put some in. It's your food!

Have family members or friends write down their favorite recipes on the blank recipe forms at the end of this chapter.

Taco meat

1 pound lean ground beef
1 small onion, chopped
1 clove garlic, minced
¾ cup water

½ teaspoon salt
3 tablespoons chili powder
1 teaspoon cumin

In a large skillet, cook ground beef with chopped onion and minced garlic until meat is thoroughly browned. Turn off stove. Drain any fat by moving beef to one side of pan, tilt pan, then spoon fat into glass jar. (Put lid on jar.) Pour water into skillet along with salt, chili powder, and cumin. Turn burner back on to medium heat. Stir meat, water, and spices together and bring to boil. Turn heat to low and simmer for 5 minutes, stirring occasionally. If mixture gets too dry, add a little more water. If the mixture is too watery, let it cook a little longer, until most of the water evaporates.

Use the taco meat in one of the recipes below. Freeze or refrigerate any leftover meat.

Taco meat recipes

Traditional tacos

Place 2–3 teaspoons of taco meat in hard or soft taco shells. Top with shredded cheese, lettuce, tomato, and sour cream. Serve with taco sauce. Note: 1 pound taco meat will make 10–12 tacos.

Burritos

Place 2–3 teaspoons of taco meat on large flour tortilla. Top with refried beans and cheese.

Taco salad

On a plate, place some shredded lettuce, crushed tortilla chips, diced tomatoes, black beans, 3 teaspoons taco meat, sour cream, and salsa.

Easy chili

1 pound lean ground beef
1 small onion, chopped
2 cloves garlic, minced
2 cans diced tomatoes—do not drain
2 cans kidney beans—do not drain
½ teaspoon salt
2 tablespoons chili powder
1 teaspoon cumin

Brown meat, onion, and garlic in large skillet. Drain excess fat. Put meat in a Crock-Pot or large pot with lid. Add tomatoes, kidney beans, and spices. Stir and heat. In Crock-Pot, cook on low for at least 3–4 hours. In pot on stove, bring to boil, then reduce heat to low; simmer for at least 1 hour, stirring occasionally. Makes 8 servings. Serve with shredded cheese.

Note: You can use leftover chili to make a taco salad. You can also serve chili over a baked potato or rice.

Two easy chicken-breast recipes

Option 1

In large, sealable plastic bag, put 3 tablespoons olive oil, 1 tablespoon Dijon mustard, 2 teaspoons lime juice, and ¼ teaspoon pepper. Seal and shake bag. Open bag and plop in 2–4 skinned chicken breast halves. Seal and shake again to coat meat with marinade. Place in refrigerator and let chill for at least 30 minutes. (You can let it marinate for up to 8 hours.)

Take out chicken breasts and discard marinade.

To grill: place chicken on heated grill and cook until meat is no longer pink. (Temperature in the middle of the breast should be 170 degrees. Depending on thickness of meat, cook 6–10 minutes per side.) To prevent burning, you may have to turn every 3 minutes.

To bake: place chicken in 9x13-inch baking dish and bake at 350 degrees for 30 minutes or until done.

Serve chicken with rice and vegetable.

Option 2

Pour 3 tablespoons of Italian dressing into a large, sealable plastic bag along with 2–4 chicken breasts. Seal bag and shake to coat meat. Place in refrigerator for at least 30 minutes. Grill or bake using directions above.

Note: Leftover chicken can be chopped and used to make chicken salads or casseroles.

More chicken recipes

Chicken salad

Toss together the following ingredients:
1 cup cooked chicken, chopped
¼ cup celery, chopped
½ cup grapes, sliced in half, or ¼ cup dried cranberries
¼ cup dry-roasted, slivered almonds or chopped pecans
1 tablespoon mayonnaise

Roasted whole chicken

Remove all packaging from whole chicken roaster or fryer. (Roaster has more meat than fryer, but either will work.) Reach inside chicken and pull out package containing the chicken heart, liver, and gizzard, as well as chicken neck. (Some people use these parts in other recipes. I discard them.) Rinse the inside and outside of the chicken. Drain water and pat outside dry.

Place chicken in roasting pan or 9x13-inch glass baking dish. Lightly spray chicken with nonstick olive-oil spray. Sprinkle lightly with salt and pepper. You can also sprinkle with a mixture of sage, oregano, and basil.

Place chicken in 350-degree oven and bake uncovered for 1½ to 2 hours, depending on size of chicken. (Temperature of thigh meat should reach 170 degrees.) If chicken is browning too quickly, cover lightly with aluminum foil for the last 15–20 minutes.

Remove cooked chicken from oven and let it sit for 10–15 minutes before slicing. Slice and serve with baked potato, wild rice, and salad.

When finished with meal, slice or pull remaining meat off chicken carcass and place in freezer baggie. Refrigerate or freeze for use in later meals.

Note: Meat from chicken can be used in casseroles, salads, chicken enchiladas, or sandwiches. Chicken carcass can be boiled to make broth.

Simple chicken broth

Place chicken carcass (or you can use any pieces of chicken meat) in large stockpot or Dutch oven. Cover with 6 cups of water. Add one washed stalk of celery with leaves, one whole peeled carrot (with top cut off), and ¼ teaspoon black pepper. Optional: add peeled onion cut in half and/or a peeled clove of garlic.

Bring to boil. Cover and turn down temperature to low. Cook for 1 hour. Remove from heat and cool a little. Remove carcass and vegetables from broth. If desired for soup, pick off any meat from chicken and put in broth.

You can continue with a soup recipe or place broth in a sealed container and refrigerate or freeze for later use. You can keep broth in the fridge for 5 days or in the freezer for 1 month. You can also freeze broth in ice-cube trays to use when recipes call for small amounts of chicken broth.

Traditional chicken noodle soup

In stockpot or Dutch oven, pour 6 cups of homemade chicken broth with meat. Add the following: 2 stalks celery, washed and chopped, and 3 large carrots, washed, peeled, and sliced. Bring broth and veggies to boil. Turn down heat to medium and cook for 20 minutes.

Return to boil and add 2 cups egg noodles. Boil over medium heat for 9–10 minutes. Stir in 1–2 cups frozen peas. Turn off heat and serve.

Note: For chicken rice soup, substitute 1 cup rice for noodles. Cook for 20 minutes over medium heat with lid on.

Essential egg recipes

Hard-boiled egg

Place however many eggs you want to boil on the bottom of a saucepan. Eggs should not be crowded or on top of one another. Cover eggs with water. Place pan on stove and turn heat to medium. When water starts to boil (bubble constantly), turn heat down slightly and cook eggs for 10 minutes. After 10 minutes, carefully drain hot water. Pour cold water over eggs, and add some ice cubes. Let eggs cool for a few minutes. Peel and use.

Note: Hard-boiled eggs can be eaten by themselves, made into egg salad, or added to other salads and recipes.

The perfect fried egg

Heat nonstick skillet over medium-high heat for 1–2 minutes. Spray with nonstick spray. (Spray should sizzle but not turn black.)

Crack 1–2 eggs quickly and carefully over skillet and let fall gently into skillet. Sprinkle with salt and pepper to taste. When most of the egg white looks solid and white in color (no longer clear), pour ¼ – ½ cup water into skillet and cover with lid. For sunny-side-up eggs (eggs with runny yolks), turn off heat and remove lid after 30 seconds. Yolk should be covered with slightly white film. Remove eggs from skillet using a rubber, slotted spatula. Serve immediately. For eggs with more solid yolks, cook covered for a little longer.

Note: According the FDA Web site, eggs should be cooked until yolks are firm to kill bacteria, unless eggs are pasteurized in-shell to destroy salmonella.

Perfect scrambled eggs

Place nonstick skillet on stove and turn on medium heat. Crack two eggs into a bowl. Add 1 tablespoon of milk or water. Stir rapidly with wire whisk or fork until mixture is evenly yellow. Add a little salt and pepper to taste. Spray skillet with nonstick spray, and immediately pour eggs into skillet. Wait 15–30 seconds, then gently push rubber spatula around skillet, lifting cooked eggs off bottom and turning uncooked eggs from the top to the skillet surface. Continue to move eggs around until completely cooked but still moist looking. Turn off heat. Sprinkle with grated cheese, if perferred. Serve immediately.

Essential omelet

Get out and set aside any of the following ingredients you want inside your omelet. The total amount of your ingredients should not exceed ¾ cup. Here are some options for omelet fillers:

Grated cheese (¼ cup) | Sliced mushrooms

Spinach	Ham, cubed
Turkey, cubed	Olives
Avocado	Diced tomato
Peppers, thinly sliced	Fresh salsa

Note: You may want to slightly cook harder vegetables like mushrooms and peppers in separate skillet. Add a little butter or olive oil to small skillet; heat; add vegetables and cook until they're slightly softened, stirring often. Remove from heat and set aside.

Place 8-inch skillet on stove and turn on medium heat. Crack two eggs into bowl, and add 2 tablespoons of water. Salt and pepper to taste. Stir eggs with a rapid motion using a whisk until mixture is evenly yellow. Place 1 teaspoon butter or margarine in skillet; quickly move it around with rubber spatula to coat bottom of skillet. Immediately pour egg mixture into skillet. Let eggs cook about 15–30 seconds, then gently move eggs away from edges while tipping skillet in various directions, allowing the uncooked mixture to flow off the top to the exposed edge. Do this until all liquid mixture is gone. Let eggs cook until they're solid but still shiny. On one half of egg surface, add your ingredients—meat first, then vegetables, then cheese. Turn off heat.

Loosen eggs around edges and flip empty half over ingredients. Set serving plate on counter. To remove omelet from pan, get skillet close to your serving plate and flip quickly onto plate.

Essential quiche

Note: Quiche can be served for breakfast, lunch, or dinner. It's a great, easy meal. Serve with fruit or a salad.

One 8-inch single piecrust, either store-bought or homemade, in pie plate

6 eggs
1½ cups milk
¼ teaspoon salt
¼ teaspoon pepper
1 cup of any combination of the following:
Cooked ham, chopped
Cooked turkey, chopped
Cooked crabmeat
Bacon, crumbled
Spinach, lightly steamed and drained
Sliced mushrooms
Onion, chopped
Broccoli, steamed and chopped
1⅓ cups grated cheese—any combination of cheddar, Colby, mozzarella, Swiss, or Monterey Jack

Preheat oven to 400 degrees. Bake empty pie shell for 7 minutes. Crack eggs into large mixing bowl, then add milk and spices. Stir rapidly with whisk until egg mixture is completely yellow. Take piecrust out of oven, and reduce oven temperature to 325. Gently spoon meat and vegetables into pie shell. Sprinkle cheese over meat and vegetables. Pour egg mixture over cheese. Place in 325-degree oven, and bake for 45 minutes or until knife inserted in center of quiche comes out clean. Let quiche cool for a few minutes before slicing.

Favorite recipes

Recipe for ______________________ Serves __________

From ____

Ingredients: ____________________________________

____

____

Directions: ____________________________________

____

____

____

____

Serving ideas: __________________________________

Recipe for ______________________ Serves __________

From ____

Ingredients: ____________________________________

____

____

Directions: ____________________________________

____

____

____

____

Serving ideas: __________________________________

Is it done?

Meat must be cooked until it reaches a certain internal temperature to kill harmful bacteria that cause food-borne illnesses. Before you serve the following foods, use an instant kitchen thermometer to make sure they've reached the following temperatures:

Chicken breasts	170 degrees F
Egg dishes	160 degrees F
Fish	145 degrees F
Ground beef	160 degrees F
Pork	160 degrees F
Steaks and roasts	145 degrees F
Whole turkey	180 degrees F

To get an accurate reading, stick the thermometer in the thickest part of the food, usually the center. Avoid touching bone, fat, or gristle. You may want to test the food in several places.

Cooking tip

It doesn't take long for peas or spinach to cook—less than 1 minute. Overcooked peas lose their bright green color, and spinach disintegrates. So add peas and spinach to a recipe at the last possible minute.

PART 8
STAYING HEALTHY

Look, life offers no guarantees.

There's no guarantee that you'll never get cancer, have a stroke, or suffer from a debilitating disease like lupus or multiple sclerosis. But your odds of recovering from whatever life throws at you are much greater if you face those challenges with a healthy body, mind, and spirit.

Disclaimer: The content in this section is provided for informational purposes only. It is not a substitute for professional medical advice or training. You should always seek professional medical advice regarding any medical question or condition.

Chapter 37

To Life, Good Health, and Happiness

How much enjoyment and satisfaction you get out of life depends on your physical, mental, and spiritual health. Life is tough, and poor health often makes a minor obstacle overwhelming. But having a strong body, a positive outlook, and deep faith helps people overcome amazing odds and walk through even horrific events with grace.

Spending time improving your physical, mental, and spiritual health pays big dividends. Good health allows you to build positive memories, strong relationships, and enduring success at whatever task God has put in front of you.

Tips for getting and staying physically healthy

- Maintain a healthy weight.
- Eat a balanced diet (see chapter 33).

- Practice good hygiene (see chapter 39).
- Be physically active—get up and do some exercise for at least thirty minutes a day.
- Get a good night's sleep—eight hours of sleep is what most adults need.
- Take care of your teeth—brush and floss daily, and see a dentist at least annually.
- Avoid high-risk behavior (sexual activity outside marriage, drug and alcohol consumption, drinking and driving, flying a kite in a lightning storm).

How calories count

3,500 unused calories = 1 pound of fat on your body
15 minutes of brisk walking = 100 calories burned
5 weeks of daily 15 minute walks = 1 pound lost

Tips for staying mentally healthy

- Take good care of your body.
- Set realistic goals.
- Surround yourself with good people.
- Learn something new.
- Help others.
- Plan your day ahead of time. (But be flexible!)
- Laugh.
- Get help when you need it.
- Pray.

- Balance work and play.
- Do something fun.

Tips on being spiritually healthy

- Be an active member of a faith community.
- Spend daily quiet time with God, and mediate on His Word
- Read the Bible.
- Pray.
- Find a spiritual mentor whom you respect.
- Serve others.
- Embrace sound spiritual teaching and godly leadership.
- Record your thoughts in a journal.
- Don't be afraid to ask questions.

Tips from others

(Have family members or friends fill these out.)

Suggestions for staying physically healthy

1. ______________________________

2. ______________________________

Suggestions for staying mentally healthy

1. ______________________________

2. ______________________________

Suggestions for staying spiritually healthy

1. ______________________________

2. ______________________________

- 15 minutes of running up stairs burns 264 calories.
- A 1-hour casual soccer game burns 493 calories.
- Playing with kids outside for an hour burns 216 calories.
- A half hour of dancing burns 185 calories.
- Walking a dog for a half hour burns 149 calories.
- Swimming for 30 minutes burns about 300 calories.
- Jumping rope for 10 minutes burns 114 calories.
- Playing a casual game of volleyball for 30 minutes burns 103 calories.
- An hour at the mall shopping and trying on clothes burns 135 calories.
- Bowling for an hour, without sitting down between turns, burns 145 calories.
- Skateboarding for 30 minutes burns about 140 calories.
- Grocery shopping, including loading groceries and putting them away, burns 90 calories per hour.

Below is a list of physical activities. Circle all that sound like fun to you.

Walking	Hiking	Roller-skating
Ice-skating	Bicycling	Gardening
Yoga	Ballroom dancing	Ballet
Modern dancing	Tennis	Softball
Golf	Coaching kids' team	Basketball
Soccer	Bowling	Lacrosse
Ping-Pong	Wrestling	Paintball
Karate	Tae kwon do	Jumping rope
Swimming	Volleyball	Airsoft

Jogging	Yardwork	Mowing grass
Stacking wood	Boxing	Weight training
Aerobics	Water aerobics	Circuit weight training
Line dancing	Swing dancing	Irish stepdancing
Walking dog	Horseback riding	Canoeing
Water-skiing	Snorkeling	Skateboarding
Kayaking	Surfing	Sailing
Hunting	Playing with kids	Washing car
Construction	Home repair	Heavy housecleaning
Auto repair	Raking leaves	Weeding
Dodgeball	Water polo	Football
Basketball	Kickboxing	Archery
Shoveling snow	Landscaping	Snowboarding
Tetherball	Badminton	Curling
Running, less than 3 miles	Walking while pushing stroller or wheelchair	Running, more than 3 miles

List one or two activities you could do on a regular basis, two to three times a week, and when you're going to do them this week.

1. ______________________________

2. ______________________________

List three activities you would like to do on a semiregular or seasonal basis and what you need to do to accomplish this goal.

1. ______________________________

2. ______________________________

3. ______________________________

Intense!

Moderately intense physical activity is any exercise that burns 3.5 to 7 calories per minute. (Examples: dancing, swimming, bicycling on flat surface, walking briskly, or golfing).

Vigorous physical activity is exercise that burns up more than 7 calories per minute. (Examples: high-impact aerobics, bicycling uphill, jogging, carrying 25 pounds up stairs, backpacking, or jumping rope).[14]

The talk test—how hard are you really exercising?

If you can talk and walk at the same time, you aren't working too hard. If you can sing and maintain your level of effort, your level of exercise is light. If you get out of breath quickly, you're probably exercising vigorously—especially if you have to stop and catch your breath.[15]

Chapter 39

Germs and Junk

Germs cause all kinds of icky illnesses (like the flu, the common cold, strep, meningitis, and the plague). These microscopic organisms cause about ten million adults in the United States to miss work annually, and each year 160,000 people in the United States die from infectious diseases, according to the CDC.

Your health depends on your ability to avoid, fight, and prevent the spread of these nasty little buggers. What are some easy, practical ways to keep germs away?

1. Wash your hands

Any time your hands are dirty—after you use the restroom, change a diaper, blow your nose, touch raw meat, handle garbage, are around sick people, or are around animals—you need to wash your hands.

Just 'cause you got 'em wet doesn't mean they're clean

To really get your hands clean . . .

- remove jewelry;
- wet your hands thoroughly with warm water;
- use soap, and scrub hands for at least 10 seconds, washing both hands and wrists;
- turn off water using a paper towel;
- dry your hands using another paper towel or air dryer; and
- don't touch any other dirty surfaces as you leave the restroom. Since studies have shown that 1 out of 5 people don't wash their hands at all after using the restroom,[16] the door handle may be the dirtiest surface of all. Use a paper towel to open the door, then throw away the towel.

2. Keep your hands (and your germs) to yourself

- Cover your mouth and nose when you sneeze or cough. Either use a tissue or cough into the crook of your elbow.
- Avoid touching your eyes, nose, or mouth.
- Stay home if you have a fever or diarrhea or if you're nauseated or vomiting.

3. Keep yourself clean

- Shower or bathe daily.
- Wash your hair at least every other day.
- Keep fingernails and toenails trimmed.
- Brush and floss your teeth at least two times a day.

Things you should never share

- Lip balm or lipstick
- Toothbrush
- Toothpaste
- Mascara
- Razor

4. Clean the space around you regularly

Germs can live on any surface for hours, if not days. That's why it's important not only to clean but also to disinfect kitchen countertops, bathrooms, and your work space. (See chapter 50 for how to actually clean.) *Disinfect* means to clean with something that kills germs, such as bleach, Lysol, or rubbing alcohol. Make sure you read the directions on the label before using any of these products.

5. Handle and prepare food correctly

Expunged sponge

Nuke damp sponges in the microwave for 1 minute or wash them in the dishwasher every night to kill growing bacteria.

Wash your hands and clean all surfaces *before* you handle any food. Make sure you wash all fruits and vegetables. Use disposable paper towels when cleaning kitchen surfaces—germs breed rapidly in damp cloth towels and sponges. (Ever take a deep whiff of a washcloth or sponge the morning after you've used it to clean? Gross!)

Also, you don't want to cross-contaminate foods (spread bacteria from one food to another). Here are some tips to help you avoid cross-contamination:

- Keep raw meat and eggs away from other foods—even in your grocery cart. Don't let the juice from raw meat or eggs drip on other foods.
- Use separate cutting boards for meat and produce.
- A plate that held raw meat, poultry, eggs, or seafood should not be used for anything else until washed and sanitized.
- Don't reuse marinades. Throw them away after one use.

- Cook foods to the proper temperature to make sure all bacteria have been killed.
- Immediately refrigerate (at a temperature of 40 degrees) food and leftovers. Perishable foods turn lethal after two hours at room temperature.

Cooling leftovers

It is not necessary to allow leftovers to cool before refrigerating. To avoid heating the refrigerator, place items in smaller containers for storage.

6. Get immunized

Getting shots may not be any fun, but neither is getting sick. Immunizations can save your life. Before you leave home, make sure you've completed all your childhood immunizations and have a record of when these immunizations took place. (See chapter 43 regarding personal health history.) The end of childhood does not mean the end of getting shots. You'll need to keep up on some immunizations as an adult. See your doctor regarding specific immunizations you may need.

Here are some adult immunizations recommended by the CDC for those 19–49 years old:

- Tetanus, diphtheria, pertussis (Td/Tdap)—once every ten years.
- Human Papillomavirus (HPV)—females, get three doses, especially if you plan to engage in any sexual activity with someone who has had any sexual contact with someone else.
- Measles, mumps, rubella (MMR)—one or two doses if you're not immune to these diseases, which can be confirmed through lab tests. If you are pregnant or can become pregnant, DO NOT get this immunization.

- Varicella (chicken pox)—two doses if you are not already immunized. If you are pregnant or can become pregnant, DO NOT get this immunization.
- Influenza (flu)—one dose annually, especially if you have a suppressed immune system, diabetes, asthma, or other chronic disorders. Check with your doctor.
- Pneumococcal (a type of pneumonia) polysaccharide vaccine (PPV)—one or two doses, especially if you have diabetes, chronic disorders of the pulmonary system, liver disease, sickle-cell anemia, HIV, cancer, or chronic renal failure.
- Hepatitis A—two doses, especially if you have chronic liver disease, engage in homosexual behavior, use illegal drugs, work in a medical research lab, or travel abroad.
- Hepatitis B—three doses, especially if you have a sexually transmitted disease (STD), renal disease, HIV, or chronic liver disease; or if you work in health care, public safety, or a correctional facility; or if you use illegal drugs, had sex with a person with Hepatitis B, had household contact with someone with Hepatitis B, or travel to other countries.
- Meningococcal (meningitis)—one or more doses, especially if you are a college student or a military recruit or if you travel abroad.

7. Use antibiotics wisely

Antibiotics are strong medicines that kill bacterial infections. But they don't treat illnesses caused by viruses. Overuse of antibiotics causes the bacteria to mutate into a germ that can no longer be treated by antibiotics. (That's bad. Very, very bad.) Plus, every time you take an antibiotic, sensitive bacteria are killed, but bad germs can be left to grow and multiply. Overuse can also make some drugs less effective.

Don't take antibiotics for . . .

- colds.
- flu.
- most coughs and bronchitis.
- sore throats (unless you have strep throat).

Always . . .

- talk to your doctor about the best treatment.
- when on an antibiotic, take as prescribed, and complete the course of treatment.
- take only antibiotics prescribed to you.
- be aware that some antibiotics decrease the effectiveness of oral contraception.

8. Take care around animals

Animals, even Fido, can pass diseases to humans. Wild animals and insects carry diseases like the plague, rabies, and Lyme disease. You can easily reduce your chances of contracting any of these illnesses by doing the following:

- Clean litter boxes daily, and thoroughly disinfect any spot where Spot did his duty in the house.
- Seal all garbage cans, and clear counters (couches, beds, etc.) of all food.
- Use insect repellent to prevent ticks and mosquitoes from biting.

- Make sure all pets are current on their vaccinations.
- Keep pets flea free.
- Wash hands after handling any animal.
- Don't try to rescue an injured wild animal yourself. Call your local animal control and let them do their job.
- Don't bring wild animals indoors and try to turn them into pets.

Chapter 40

What You Drink

You are 66 percent liquid—specifically, water. Humans can't live without water for more than a week. So what do you need to know about what you drink?

How much water do I need to drink every day?

Eight glasses, every day. More if you exercise or work outside or if you're sick.

Why do I need water, anyway?

Your body needs water to function. Water is a major player in your blood, digestive system, body joints, and temperature regulation.

What happens if I don't drink enough water?

You become dehydrated and you'll suffer varying degrees of effects depending on how dehydrated you are.

Mild dehydration symptoms: dry mouth, thirst, dizziness, feeling hungry, headaches, tiredness, loss of concentration, sunken eyes, dark yellow urine.

Moderate dehydration: substantial loss of strength and endurance, heat exhaustion, dry and wrinkled skin, reduced blood pressure, fatigue, constipation, peeing only three times in twenty-four hours.

Severe dehydration: 10 percent or greater reduction in body weight due to lack of water, seizures, brain damage, loss of consciousness, extreme anxiety, rapid breathing.

How can I tell if I'm drinking enough water?

You're drinking enough water if you're not thirsty and your urine is clear or only slightly yellow.

Can I drink too much water?

It's uncommon, but you can develop water intoxication from drinking too much water at one time. Try to keep water intake to no more than one to two cups in a given hour. Water intoxication leads to kidney failure and can be fatal.

Does everything I drink count as water?

No. Coffee, tea, diet drinks, caffeinated beverages, and alcohol are diuretics—meaning they actually reduce the amount of water in your body. (By the way, the nicotine in cigarettes and other tobacco products is also a diuretic.)

I feel bloated and puffy. Should I drink less water?

Actually, if you aren't drinking enough water, your body will kick into survival mode and start retaining water, up to a gallon a day. Drinking the proper amount of water will actually help you lose this extra "water weight" as well as the bloated feeling.

Soda facts

Drinking one can of soda a day can add fifteen pounds a year to your weight.

But diet soda may not be any better: Surprisingly, studies have shown that diet drinks don't help people lose weight. In fact, according to a study at the University of Texas, people drinking only diet soft drinks had a higher risk of obesity.[17]

PART 9
I DON'T FEEL SO GOOD

Few things can make you feel more homesick (no pun intended) than being sick for the first time on your own. Having chills, a fever, and nausea alone in your apartment or dorm can make the strongest of us cry, "I want my mommy!"

Don't let the throes of illness make you revert to childhood. You're an adult, and you can make it through this. Just remember:

- Get plenty of rest.
- Drink lots of water.
- Go to the doctor, if necessary (see chapter 41).
- Then call your mom—not because you need to but because she needs to feel needed.

Disclaimer: The content in this section is provided for informational purposes only. It is not a substitute for professional medical advice or training. You should always seek professional medical advice regarding any medical question or condition.

Chapter 41

When to Go to the Doctor

With the cost of health care these days, it's wise to know when you really need to see a doctor or go to the hospital.

If you're experiencing any of the following symptoms, go to the hospital emergency room NOW! If you can't get yourself to the hospital, call 911.

- Severe bleeding, including bleeding that will not stop when pressure is applied
- Difficulty breathing
- Head trauma
- Seizures or convulsions
- Dehydration
- Chest pain

- Suddenly becoming confused or disoriented
- Rapid heartbeat
- Very high fever, over 104° F
- Broken bone
- Severe pain
- Change in vision
- Persistent diarrhea or vomiting
- Fainting, suddenly dizzy or weak
- Vomiting blood
- Abnormal and heavy vaginal bleeding
- After any auto accident
- Bright red blood in bowel movement
- Weakness on one side of face or in arm or leg
- Slurred speech
- Severe headache
- Pain in left arm, neck, and jaw
- Poisoning
- Suicidal or homicidal feelings
- Loss of consciousness
- Overdose of medication

If you are experiencing any of the following symptoms, call your doctor right away, and see your doctor within twenty-four hours. If you can't get in to see your doctor, go to an urgent care center.

- Persistent vomiting, can't keep any food down
- Fever (If you have a temperature of 102° F or higher, see

the doctor right away. If your temperature is lower than 102° F, go to the doctor if you have a fever for more than forty-eight hours).

- Slight but persistent difficultly breathing—see doctor right away
- Excessive sleepiness, fatigue, or confusion
- Abdominal pain, if it is causing you to double over or if it is persistent
- Bloody stool
- Significant pain
- Pinkeye (conjunctivitis)—eye is swollen, red, or feels like it has sand in it
- Persistent feelings of depression—feeling down, blue, or lethargic
- Severe sore throat or painful swallowing
- Limping
- Earache
- Persistent headaches
- Rash
- Coughing up dark yellow or green mucus
- Persistent difficulty focusing on a task
- Burning or pain when urinating
- Abnormal discharge from vagina or penis
- Persistent itching around genitals
- Abnormal vaginal bleeding

- Abnormal menstrual periods, either too frequent or too far apart (periods should occur every twenty-seven to thirty-one days)
- Abnormal lumps in breasts

What's the difference?

- An emergency room is for severe, life-threatening situations.
- An urgent care center is for injury or illness that is not life-threatening but needs same-day medical attention.

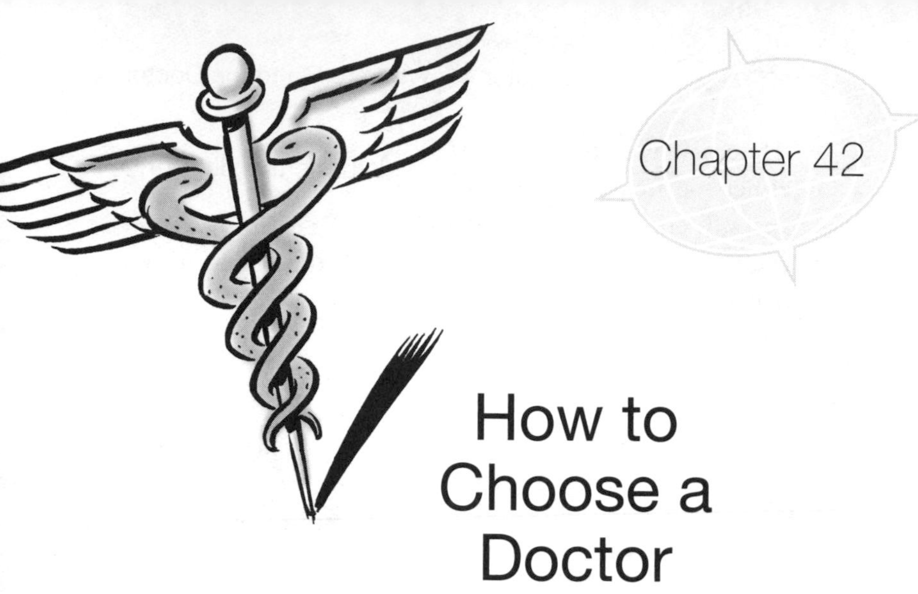

Chapter 42

How to Choose a Doctor

You may have gone to your family's doctor throughout your life. Or perhaps your primary physician has always been a pediatrician. Now that you're an adult, you'll want to find a primary care physician you're comfortable with and can trust. Your primary care physician, more than likely a family practice doctor or internist, is the doctor you visit when you're sick and for regular annual physicals. If your symptoms suggest the need for a specialist, your primary care physician will refer you to a specialist.

What to look for in a doctor

If you have insurance, check what doctors are in your plan's network of physicians. If you have no health insurance, go to http://www.ask.hrsa.gov/pc/ and search for free medical clinics in your area. Most clinics operate on a walk-in basis, meaning you probably will not get a choice which doctor you see.

1. *Once you have a list of potential doctors, check out their qualifications and background*. You can do this online:

- Administrators in Medicine, www.docboard.org
- CertiFACTS (American Board of Medical Specialties), www.certifacts.org
- American Medical Association, www.ama-assn.org

2. *Choose up to three doctors with the best qualifications and reputation*. Find out which hospitals the doctor uses by calling the doctor's office. Is there a hospital you prefer?

While you're on the phone with the office staff, ask them the following questions:

- Is the doctor taking new patients?
- How long until I can get a new-patient appointment?
- Once I'm an established patient, how quickly can I get a routine appointment?
- How long is the typical wait to see the doctor?
- What are the office hours?
- If my doctor isn't available, is there another doctor on staff who would see me?
- Is there a nurse on staff whom I can call for medical advice during regular office hours?
- Is the doctor available by phone for after-hours emergencies?
- Do I get billed if I have to cancel an appointment?

3. *Schedule a new-patient appointment with the doctor that seems to suit you best.* This does not obligate you to choose this doctor as your primary care physician.
4. *While the doctor is checking you out, check him or her out (professionally speaking):*

- Was the doctor respectful?
- Did the doctor encourage you to ask questions?
- Did the doctor listen to you?
- Did the doctor answer your questions clearly?
- Were you comfortable around the doctor?
- Did the doctor spend enough time with you?
- Did the doctor address all of your health problems?
- Did the doctor give you enough information regarding your health issues?
- Did the doctor talk to you about prevention as well as taking care of existing symptoms?
- Did the doctor seem concerned about your overall health?

If the answer to all the above questions is yes, then you've found yourself a doctor. If not, go back to your list of candidates and make an appointment with another physician.

What to bring to the doctor's office

- Your personal and family health history (see chapter 43).
- A list of the medications you are currently taking.
- A list of what you are allergic to, including medications, foods, animals, dust, etc. Know what type of allergic reac-

tion you've experienced when exposed to the items on your list (e.g., hives, sneezing, wheezing, and swelling).

- A list of any natural or alternative medicines or treatments you use.

Questions you should ask your doctor

(Don't be afraid to write down questions ahead of time or take notes during your visit.)

- What is the name of my illness? What exactly is it?
- How long should my recovery take?
- Besides medication, what else can I do to speed up my healing?
- When should I feel better?
- What if I feel worse?
- What can I do to prevent this from happening again?
- Are there symptoms you would want me to call you about right away?

Don't wait until you're sick to find a doctor!

Most doctors insist that you have a new-patient appointment with them before they will see you for a regular appointment. The new-patient appointment allows the physician to get to know you and the status of your physical health. You don't have to be sick for a new-patient appointment. In fact, it's better if you're well so that the doctor can get a baseline reading on your blood pressure, weight, temperature, and overall health. Doctors schedule longer appointments with new patients and usually have a limited number of appointments available. Don't be surprised if you have to wait four to eight weeks to get in to see the doctor. For this reason, it's important that once you choose a doctor, you call and schedule your initial appointment as soon as possible.

- If I take any prescribed medication, what is considered a normal side effect? What is considered a dangerous side effect?
- Should I make a follow-up appointment? If so, when?

What do all those initials mean, anyway?

Your primary health care provider probably will have one of the following sets of initials behind his or her name. What do those initials really mean?

- M.D.—This person went to a four-year medical school and is a Doctor of Medicine. After residency at a hospital, MDs usually choose a specialty such as heart surgery, obstetrics, or internal medicine. MDs can perform surgery, prescribe medicine, and deliver babies.
- D.O.—This person went to a four-year medical school and is a Doctor of Osteopathy. DOs do their residency at a community hospital or doctor's office. DOs focus on healing and treating the whole patient rather than focusing on one system of the body. DOs can prescribe medicine, perform surgery, and deliver babies.
- N.P.—An NP is a Nurse Practitioner (a nurse who has an advanced nursing degree). NPs can diagnose illnesses and prescribe medicine. NPs cannot perform surgery, and they usually work under a doctor's supervision.
- P.A.—A Physician's Assistant has a minimum of two years of medical training at the college level, although most PAs have a four-year degree. PAs work under the supervision of a medical doctor and can diagnose and supervise treatment of patients. Most states allow PAs to prescribe medication. They cannot perform surgery.

Chapter 43

Your Personal and Family Health History

Your health background, along with the health history of your siblings, parents, grandparents, aunts, and uncles, helps your doctor accurately diagnose your condition, prescribe the correct treatment, be on the lookout for certain diseases, and avoid making dangerous mistakes.

For example, if your mother and grandmother both had diabetes, your doctor would pay special attention to preventing and diagnosing diabetes in you. If your sister had cancer, the doctor would be on the lookout for any signs of that disease in you.

More than likely, your parent always filled out the family health history for you at the doctor's office. You may only have a vague idea of your own health history, much less Aunt Marge's.

Before you leave home, have your family members fill out the health forms below. You can download the form at http://www

.simonsays.com/content/book.cfm?tab=1&pid=614860&agid=38. At the very least, it will prevent you from looking like a complete idiot the first time you go to the doctor by yourself. It could also save your life.

Your health history form

Full name ________________________________ Sex M F

Date of birth ______________ Age ____ Blood type ______

Current medications and natural supplements and why you take them

____

____

I am allergic to (include type of allergic reaction) ____________

____

____

Birth defects _____________________________________

____

____

Developmental disabilities (include physical and learning disabilities)

____

____

Surgeries (list type, date, and reason for surgery) ____________

____

____

Hospitalizations (dates and reasons)_____________________

____

____

Injuries, conditions, or illnesses (type and date) ______________

____

____

If female, list all live births, miscarriages, stillbirths, and infant deaths with date and cause, if known ____________________

____

____

Do you wear glasses or contacts? Y N Do you smoke? Y N
Were you raised in a home with a smoker? Y N
Do you drink alcohol? Y N How often? ____________

Do you, or have you ever, taken illegal drugs? Y N
What kind? ____________________________________

____

Immunization record (list dates for vaccines you have received)

Hepatitis B (HBV) ____________, __________, ________

Polio (IPV) _____________, ______________, ___________

Haemophilus influenzae type B (Hib) _________, ________,
____

Diphtheria, tetanus, pertussis (DTaP, Td) ______, ________,
____

Measles, mumps and rubella (MMR)

Chickenpox (Varicella, VZV) ________________

Pneumococcal disease (Prenar) __________, _____________,
____

Hepatitis A ___________________

Other doctors or specialists I see (list names and reasons you see them)

____

____

____

____

Family health history

Parents

Name of mother ________________________ Date__________

Date of birth ________________ Date of death ________________

Health conditions (please include date condition began)

Diseases and medical conditions ________________________

____

Developmental disabilities (list all, including learning and physical disabilities) ______________________________

____

Surgeries (list types, reasons, and dates) ____________________

____

Allergies ____________________________________

Miscarriages, stillbirths, or infant deaths (list date and cause, if known) __________________________________

____

Do you smoke? Y N

Do you live with someone who smokes? Y N
Are you overweight? Y N
Do you work or live around chemicals/toxins? Y N
Do you drink alcohol? Y N How often? ______________
Countries of origin (Where did your family members come from?)

____

____

Name of father ______________________ Date__________

Date of birth ______________ Date of death ______________

Health conditions (please include date condition began)

Diseases and medical conditions ______________________

____

Developmental disabilities (list all, including learning and physical disabilities) ______________________________

____

____

Surgeries (list types, reasons, and dates) ________________

____

Allergies ______________________________________

Do you smoke? Y N
Do you live with someone who smokes? Y N
Are you overweight? Y N
Do you work or live around chemicals/toxins? Y N
Do you drink alcohol? Y N How often? ______________
Countries of origin (Where did your family members come from?)

____

____

Other family members

Include all siblings, grandparents, aunts, uncles, great-grandparents, great-aunts and great-uncles, if possible. Write the family health history for those listed above. Download this form at http://www.simonsays.com/content/book.cfm?tab=1&pid=614860&agid=38.

Name________________________________ Date__________

Relationship to you ____________________________Sex M F

Date of birth ______________ Date of death ______________

Health conditions (please include date condition began)

Diseases and medical conditions ________________________

____

____

____

Developmental disabilities (list all, including learning and physical disabilities) ___________________________________

____

____

Surgeries (list types, reasons, and dates) __________________

____

____

____

Allergies ______________________________________

Miscarriages, stillbirths, or infant deaths (list date and cause, if known) ____

____

Chapter 44

Health Insurance Options

You're over eighteen, you've left home, and your parents' health insurance no longer covers you. What do you do? Go without? According to the U.S. Census Bureau, 30 percent of adults aged eighteen to twenty-four have no health insurance. Living without some type of health insurance is a really bad idea. So, what are your options?

Types of insurance

Fee-for-service

- Offers choice of doctors and hospitals.
- You can go to a hospital in any part of the country.
- Insurance company pays part of your medical bills.

- You pay a premium, deductible, and the portion of your bill the insurance company did not pay.
- Either you or the doctor's office fills out and files insurance claims.
- Fee-for-service is available as individual or group insurance.

Health Maintenance Organization (HMO)

- Doctor and hospital choices are limited to those under contract with the HMO.
- HMO typically covers preventive care (such as immunizations and physicals).
- HMOs pay doctors and hospitals a fixed fee.
- You pay a premium and a small co-pay.
- You usually don't have to fill out insurance claims.
- HMOs are available as individual or group insurance.

Preferred Provider Organizations (PPO)

- A PPO is a combination of fee-for-service and an HMO.
- You have a limited number of doctors and hospitals from which to choose.
- You are required to choose a primary care physician.
- PPO covers most preventive care.
- You can use doctors who are not part of the plan, but the insurance company will only pay part of the medical bill.
- Insurance claims are usually filed only when you use a doctor outside of the plan network.

- You pay a premium and small co-payments, and you may have a deductible.
- PPOs are available as individual or group insurance.

Short-term health insurance

- Plans cover only one to thirty-six months.
- Policies can be purchased in one-month increments.
- Plans do not cover preexisting conditions.
- You have choice of doctors and hospitals.
- Insurance does not typically pay for preventive care.
- You pay premium and deductible.
- You must be in good health to qualify for most short-term plans.
- Short-term plans are available to individuals and families.

Catastrophic health insurance

- Insurance pays for only major hospital and medical expenses.
- You pay a premium, a deductible, prescription costs, and costs of routine doctor's office visits.
- Usually you or the hospital file a claim.
- Coverage is available to individuals and families.

Student health insurance

- Policies are offered to students by most colleges and universities.
- Usually you must go to a medical health clinic on campus.

- Policy usually includes catastrophic health insurance.
- You pay a low premium.
- Insurance may cover hospital and out-of-town medical expenses.
- No paperwork when you use a clinic, but a claim probably needs to be filed for hospital and out-of-town expenses.
- Policies are available only to individuals. Some colleges or universities offer reduced-cost family insurance policies through an outside vendor, such as Blue Cross Blue Shield or Kaiser Permanente.

Medicaid

- Medicaid is a federally and state-funded health insurance program.
- To qualify for Medicaid, you must have a low income or be blind or disabled.
- You may pay a small deductible.
- Choices of doctors and hospitals may be limited.
- Medicaid covers preventative as well as hospital care.
- Coverage is available only to individuals.

Disability insurance

- This is insurance to replace your income in the case of a long-term illness or injury that prevents you from working.
- It does not cover the cost of rehabilitation.
- A claim has to be filed.
- Policies are available to groups or individuals.

Costs of medical care

Average doctor's office visit	$87
Average emergency room visit	$840
Average knee surgery	$3,538
Average MRI of brain	$1,840[18]
Head injury from car accident	$45,000
Serious case of pneumonia	$75,000[19]

Assessing your health care needs

Everyone has different health care needs, based on age, occupation, and income. Before you go shopping for health insurance, ask yourself the following questions:

1. What does your health insurance really need to cover? (Check all that apply.)

☐	Hospital visits	☐	Surgery
☐	Doctor's office visits	☐	Medical tests
☐	Prescriptions	☐	Immunizations
☐	Maternity care	☐	Vision care
☐	Dental care	☐	Home health care
☐	Other ____________		

2. What is the maximum deductible that you can pay? (You'll need to keep this money set aside.) $ ______________________

3. What is the maximum premium you can pay monthly?

   $ ________________

4. Do you want to file your own insurance claims?

   ☐ Yes ☐ No

5. Do you need insurance that covers medical expenses in other cities? ☐ Yes ☐ No

6. Do you want a choice of doctors/hospitals? ☐ Yes ☐ No

7. Do you need your plan to cover a particular doctor or hospital?

☐ Yes ☐ No

If yes, which?____________________________________

Insurance terms

- *Premium:* the cost of purchasing health insurance plan. Usually paid monthly.
- *Deductible:* the amount you must pay toward medical expenses before your health insurance will pay anything. If your deductible is $1,000, then each year you must pay for the first $1,000 of your medical bills before your health insurance kicks in.
- *Co-pay:* a small flat fee you pay every time you receive medical services (example: $15 per doctor's office visit, $50 for each trip to the emergency room). Your health insurance pays the rest of the bill.
- *Group insurance:* health insurance purchased through an employer or professional organization. Employer may pay all or part of the premium. You may pay deductible and co-pays. Coverage could be limited to only yourself. Insurance for your dependents (spouse, children) may be optional.
- *Individual insurance:* health insurance you purchase yourself for you and/or your family. You pay premiums, deductibles, and co-pays.
- *Preexisting condition:* a health problem or condition you had before you purchased the health insurance policy.

Worksheet for comparing health insurance policies

Download form at http://www.simonsays.com/content/book.cfm?tab=1&pid=614860&agid=38

	Company 1	Company 2	Company 3
Name of company			
Monthly premium			
Deductible			
Co-pays			
What is covered?			
What is not covered?			
Do you have a choice of doctors/hospitals?			
What hospitals are included in the plan network?			
What or how many doctors are in the plan network?			
Will I be assigned a primary-care physician?			
Do I need a referral to see a specialist?			

Annual limits of coverage			
Lifetime limits of coverage			
Does policy cover any preexisting condition you may have?			
Is there a waiting period before coverage begins?			

Chapter 45

First-Aid Kits: What You Should Have at Home and in Your Car

At home

A first-aid kit comes in handy for household accidents—and such accidents *will* happen. Store all of your first-aid supplies in one specific place in your home: in a medicine cabinet; in a shoebox in a closet; or somewhere else that's safe, dry, and out of the reach of children.

Items to include in a basic first-aid kit

- First-aid manual
- Antiseptic wipes
- Antibiotic cream
- Adhesive bandages in various sizes
- Sterile gloves (latex or vinyl)
- Soap
- Hydrogen peroxide
- Burn ointment

- Eye-wash solution
- Gauze pads
- Tweezers
- Scissors
- Pain reliever/fever reducer (like acetaminophen or ibuprofen)
- Insect sting relief ointment or pads
- Anti-itch cream (for poison ivy or bug bites)
- Thermometer
- Stretch gauze bandage roll (to wrap sprains)
- Antidiarrheal medication
- Antihistamine
- Laxative
- Antacid
- Hand sanitizer
- Instant ice packs
- Activated charcoal (to use if advised by the Poison Control Center)

Other emergency items you should have on hand

- Flashlight with extra batteries
- Duct tape
- Paper cups
- Battery-operated radio with extra batteries
- Blanket
- Bottled water
- Fire extinguisher
- Matches
- Candles

In your car

Accidents don't just happen at home. They can happen when you're out on the road, too. That's why you should always keep a small first-aid kit in your car. Make sure you store your first-aid kit in a waterproof container, such as a tackle box or extra-sturdy, sealable plastic bag.

Items to include in the first-aid kit in your car

- First-aid manual
- Adhesive bandages
- Antiseptic wipes
- Antihistamine cream
- Instant cold pack
- Sterile gloves (latex or vinyl)
- Eye-wash solution
- Insect sting relief ointment or pads
- Antihistamine
- Pencil and small pad of paper
- List of emergency phone numbers
- Stretch gauze bandage roll
- Hand sanitizer
- Antibiotic cream
- Pocket knife with scissors and tweezers
- Extra prescription medication (especially if you're going on a trip)
- Pain reliever/fever reducer (like acetaminophen or ibuprofen)
- Sunscreen
- A couple of energy bars
- If female, a few sanitary napkins

Other emergency items you should always have in your car

(See complete list in chapter 30)

- Flashlight with extra batteries
- Bottled water
- Good map/atlas
- Blanket
- Cell phone and charger
- Tissues
- Roll of paper towels

Emergency numbers for home or on the road

Post these numbers near a phone or another obvious place at home.

In your car, put the list inside your glove compartment or first-aid kit in a sealable plastic bag so it doesn't get damaged.

Also, list any known allergies or medical conditions of you and your family/roommates.

Emergency numbers

Emergency medical services 911

Poison Control Center 1-800-222-1222

National Suicide Prevention Lifeline, 1-800-273-TALK (8255)

Hospital emergency room ______________________________

Fire department ______________________________

Police department ______________________________

Your doctor ______________________________

Your pharmacy ______________________________

Your home ______________________________

Your employer/school and contact person ______________________________

____

Emergency contact (parent, roommate, neighbor)—list home, cell, and work numbers ______________________________

____

Your church/pastor ______________________________

Veterinarian (if you have a pet) ______________________________

Known allergies/medical conditions ______________________________

Make a date to check the dates

Set aside a specific date every year (say December 31) to go through your medicine cabinet and first-aid kits to check the expiration dates on all medications and medical supplies. Throw away expired items and replace them with new ones.

Chapter 46

Basic First Aid

Each year about 20,000 people die from unintentional accidents in the home. Whether you've just mistaken your thumb for the carrot you were slicing or your roommate just fell off a ladder, you should be a good scout and be prepared.

Taking a first-aid course from the Red Cross or other community resource equips you to respond correctly to an emergency situation. Visit www.redcross.org to find your local Red Cross chapter and the training they offer.

First response

How you respond to any type of emergency is critical for your safety and the safety of others. It doesn't matter if a bee just stung you or your friend is choking on your pasta bake, follow these basic guidelines:

- Don't panic. Hyperventilating or fainting is never helpful.
- Think. Is the situation around you safe? Is the place where you (or another injured person) are located dangerous (example: burning building, car's about to explode, at the bottom of the pool)?
- If yes, then MOVE! Get yourself and anyone else you can out of harm's way.
- If no, but you or someone else is seriously hurt, call 911. Follow instructions below for "big" emergencies.
- If no, but you or someone else is "a little" hurt, follow instructions below for "little" emergencies. Remember: "little" emergencies can still be life-threatening, depending on the situation and the victim. (Example: If a person stung by a bee is allergic to bees, the sting can cause him or her to swell and have difficulty breathing. A small incident just turned into a life-threatening emergency.)

Basic first-aid tips for "big" emergencies

Person is unconscious

- Call 911.
- If the person is not breathing, perform rescue breathing.
- If the person has no heartbeat, perform CPR, if trained.

Person is in shock

Signs of shock: pale complexion; shaking; cold, clammy skin; confusion; nausea

- Call 911.
- Have person lie down.

- Cover person with blanket.
- Give person some water, as long as you're sure he or she doesn't have any stomach injuries.

Person is bleeding

- Call 911.
- Put on sterile gloves or use a clean plastic bag to cover your hands.
- Place clean cloth or bandage directly over wound.
- Press down with your fingers or hand.
- If that doesn't work, wrap a belt, tie, or strip of cloth around the cloth or bandage and tighten. Don't make it too tight. You don't want to totally cut off the circulation . . .
- unless the wound is bleeding profusely and you can't get it to stop. In this case, tie a band of cloth or rope very tightly right above the wound. This is called a tourniquet, and it should be used only in very dire circumstances. Complications include sever tissue damage that might even require amputation of the treated limb. DO NOT remove the tourniquet. Only a doctor should do so.

Person is burned

- If person is badly burned, call 911.
- Immediately put burned area in cool tap water or gently place a cool, wet towel on it for at least twenty minutes. DO NOT put ice or anything greasy on a burn.
- Look at the burn and decide whether you need to seek medical treatment (see sidebar "How bad is the burn?").

How bad is the burn?

Burn severity is assessed by degrees:

- First-degree burn—red skin, no blistering, no skin removed
- Second-degree burn—red skin with blister
- Third-degree burn—no blister, because top layers of skin are gone

Which burns require a doctor's visit?

- Large burns
- Facial burns bigger than a quarter, no matter what degree of burn
- Third-degree burns

Person hurt back, neck, or spine

- Call 911.
- DO NOT move the person unless he or she is in a very dangerous place. Any damage done to the spinal cord is serious and permanent.
- DO NOT twist the person. Keep neck and torso as straight as possible.
- If you MUST move the person, pull in a direction that keeps the neck, torso, and spine straight. Pull from shirt collar, if possible. If not, pull body from either the feet or from under both arms.

Person is choking

- Ask the person if he or she is choking.
- If the person is able to speak, let the person try unblocking his or her own airway by coughing. Stay with the person until he or she is all right. Do not hit the person on the back or give him or her something to drink.

- If the person cannot speak, or if the person starts to turn blue, call 911. Attempt the Heimlich maneuver.

The Heimlich maneuver for choking adults

A choking victim can't speak or breathe and needs your help immediately. Follow these steps to help a choking victim:

1. From behind, wrap your arms around the victim's waist.
2. Make a fist and place the thumb side of your fist against the victim's upper abdomen, below the rib cage and above the navel.
3. Grasp your fist with your other hand and press into their upper abdomen with a quick upward thrust. Do not squeeze the rib cage; confine the force of the thrust to your hands.
4. Repeat until object is expelled.[20]

Note: Performing the Heimlich maneuver incorrectly can hurt chest, ribs, and internal organs. Be careful!

Basic first-aid tips for "little" emergencies

Sprains

- Put ice on swelling immediately.
- Go to the doctor or urgent care center.

Bug bites or stings

- Remove any visible stinger.
- Apply ice.
- Call 911 or go to the hospital emergency room if breathing becomes difficult or major swelling occurs.

Colds or sore throats

- Drink more water, and take it easy.
- Wash your hands often.
- If you have a stiff neck or a temperature over 102° F, go to the emergency room.
- If you have a very sore throat, severe ear pain, or sinus pain, see a doctor.

Stomach bug

- Drink small sips of clear soda or water every five to ten minutes.
- Once vomiting stops, eat small portions of food such as toast, bananas, clear soups, rice, or crackers for the next twenty-four hours.
- If you vomit repeatedly and have a temperature over 102° F or a stiff neck, go to the emergency room.

Diarrhea

- If you experience diarrhea once or twice, just drink clear liquids until the diarrhea goes away.
- You can try over-the-counter diarrhea medicine—follow directions on label.
- If you have diarrhea for more than three days, have a temperature over 102° F, are in extreme pain, or have bloody or black stools, see a doctor.

Where to find first-aid instructions on the Web

- www.redcross.org/static/file_cont4913_lang0_1727.pdf
- www.redcross.org/static/file_cont5294_lang0_1934.pdf
- www.band-aid.com (under "First Aid Guide")
- www.mayoclinic.com/health/FirstAidIndex/FirstAidIndex

PART 10
DUST BUNNIES AND THE SOCK MONSTER

Ahhh. Nothing better than a clean house to live in and clean clothes to wear. If only you didn't have to do the work to make it that way. But keeping clean is a matter of routine. If you do a little every day, keeping the dust bunny population under control *is* possible.

Chapter 47

Divide and Conquer (Laundry)

When the phrase "necessary evil" was coined, I'm convinced the person was referring to laundry. You might get away with not dusting for a decade or not vacuuming for a month. But try that with laundry, and anytime you're in public, people will assume you're panhandling.

The only way to avoid doing laundry every other day is to have more clothes. Space and money usually eliminate the option of having 365 pairs of underwear. So plan on setting aside a couple of hours a week to do laundry. But use the time to your advantage. If you're a social person, find "the" Laundromat and go late Saturday morning to hang. If solitude is more your style, an early weekday morning with book and latte in hand might be just the thing.

Essential laundry supplies

- 2 large laundry bags: 1 for light colors, 1 for dark colors
- 1 small laundry bag for delicates
- 1 large basket to carry folded clothes
- Laundry detergent
- Stain-removal stick or spray
- Detergent designed for delicates
- Drying rack

Laundry basics

1. Divide your clothes into the following piles.

a. White/light-colored cottons—T-shirts, socks, underwear, towels

b. Light-colored casual wear—blouses, shirts, slacks, dresses

c. Dark-colored cottons—jeans, sweats, T-shirts, socks, underwear, towels

d. Dark-colored casual wear—blouses, shirts, slacks, dresses

e. Delicates—sweaters, bras, nicer blouses, swimsuits

f. Dry clean only—items marked on tag as "Dry Clean Only," such as suits, ties, dressy clothes

Note: If you have small piles, you can combine piles A and B for one load and wash on the warm/cold setting. Piles C and D can be washed together on the cold/cold setting.

2. Pretreat stains.

Before washing, rub small amount of detergent on spot, or treat with stain-removal product.

Stain solutions

Before washing clothes, pretreat these stains:

- blood—with hydrogen peroxide.
- ink—with rubbing alcohol.
- sweat—with vinegar.
- lipstick—with petroleum jelly.

3. Treat delicates delicately.

Hand-wash sweaters, bras, swimsuits, and other delicates using a small amount of detergent specifically for delicates, such as Woolite. New items that are red or brightly colored should be washed separately. Hang hand-washed items on drying rack.

4. Wash clothes.

- Set laundry machine to proper setting, and turn on.
- Pour detergent into water .
- Add clothes, distributing them evenly.

Laundry Machine Settings

	Clothing type	**Water temperature**	**Wash cycle**
1	White/light cottons	Hot/cold	Regular
2	Light-colored casual	Warm/cold	Permanent press
3	Dark-colored cottons	Warm/cold	Regular
4	Dark-colored casual	Cold/cold	Permanent press
5	Delicates	Cold/cold	Delicate

5. Dry clothes.

- To reduce wrinkles, shake out clothing before putting in dryer.

- Dark and light cotton clothes: dry on regular setting.
- Dark and light casual clothes: dry on permanent press setting.
- Be sure to empty lint from lint trap before starting dryer.
- Add a dryer sheet to eliminate static cling and wrinkles.

WARNING!

Wash all red, dark, or bright clothes separately the first time you wash them to prevent their fading onto all your other clothes. Better yet, before you wash a new item, set the colors so they won't bleed by placing the item in a bucket of water with one cup of white vinegar added. Soak three to four hours. Wash as normal. (You still shouldn't wash them with light colors.)

If you do happen to throw in your new red jersey with your white/light cottons and turn your undies a nice shade of pink, don't put them in the dryer. Wash them again with a cup of nonchlorine bleach or a cup of white vinegar.

6. Fold and hang clothes.

- Fold and hang clothes immediately after drying to prevent wrinkles.
- Put clothes away promptly for the same reason.
- Put a dryer sheet in your dresser drawers to keep clothes smelling fresh.

7. Take "dry clean only" items to a dry cleaner.

- Your "dry clean only" clothes probably can be worn more than once between cleanings.

- Don't wait until the last minute to drop off your dry cleaning.
- The turnaround time for dry cleaning is usually twenty-four to forty-eight hours.
- Keep in mind that dry cleaning is expensive.

DON'T WASH!

My dry-clean-only items:

____

____

____

____

____

____

Tips for avoiding the iron

I hate ironing. It's true. So true that I've made it a goal to eliminate the need for ironing from my life and yours! So let's recap ways you can avoid the need for this dreaded task:

- Shake out washed clothing before putting it in the dryer.
- Add a dryer sheet.
- Fold and hang clothes immediately after drying.
- Bring hangers to the Laundromat so you can hang clothes right out of the dryer. This will not only save you from wrinkles, it'll save time too!

Suggestions from home

Detergent ______________________________

For delicates ______________________________

Softener/dryer sheets______________________________

Stain remover ______________________________

Laundromat tips

- Bring something to do.
- Stay at the Laundromat with your clothes.
- Drying takes longer than washing.
- You'll find more open machines during off-peak times like early in the morning or at mealtimes.

Chapter 48

The Things You Must Clean

Mom always told you to clean your room, but now you have an entire place to clean on your own. And what did she really mean by "clean," anyway?

Here are the places and items in your house that you'll need to clean regularly, from top to bottom:

Ceiling—dust off any spiderwebs every two weeks.

Walls—wash at least a couple of times a year.

Windows—wash inside and out at least once a year.

Furniture/upholstery—dust hard surfaces once a week, vacuum fabric or leather furniture every week.

Trash cans—clean and disinfect trash cans every two weeks.

Baseboards (you know, the short board that runs along your floor at the bottom of the wall)—wash at least three or four times a year.

Floors—clean all floors at least twice a week, kitchen and bathroom floors more often.

- Hardwood floors—wash only with water or water and vinegar as needed.
- Carpet—steam-clean carpets once a year; vacuum weekly, more often if needed.
- Tile—wash with warm water or water with vinegar as needed.
- Linoleum—wash with warm water or water with vinegar as needed.

Kitchen

- Surfaces—disinfect every day; clean up immediately after preparing food.
- Refrigerator—toss out old food and leftovers once a week, clean fridge every three months.
- Stove/oven—wipe down surfaces after every use; clean oven three times a year (more often if needed).
- Microwave—wipe down inside at least twice a week.
- Cabinets—wipe down once a week.

Bathroom

- Disinfect all surfaces every day
- Scrub toilet, sink, and shower once a week.
- Clean floors once a week

Note: The more people you have using one bathroom, the more often you'll need to clean it to prevent the spread of germs.

Office/computer area

- Clean computer once a year.
- Dust weekly.
- Clear, organize, and dust office furniture once a week.

Garage/carport—sweep every two weeks or as needed.

Porches/patios and decks—every two weeks, sweep floors and sweep off all spiderwebs on walls or ceilings.

How often?

"Wash walls a couple of times a year" is a general guideline. If it's dirty, clean it. Clean spills, messes, and any of Fido's vomit or "mistakes" immediately. Don't wait six months to wipe the spaghetti sauce off the wall.

Chapter 49

Essential Cleaning Supplies

Basic cleaning essentials

- Vacuum, if you have carpet
- Dustpan
- Paper towels
- Disinfectant
- Trash can
- Good doormats, if you have exterior doors
- Broom or electric sweeper, if you have hard flooring
- A few rags
- Dusting cloths
- Glass cleaner
- Trash bags

Basic bathroom cleaning essentials

- Toilet brush with caddy
- Paper towels
- Rags
- Glass cleaner

- Disinfectant (spray or liquid)
- Squeegee (if you have a shower)
- Bucket
- Disinfectant wipes (for easy cleaning)
- Trash can
- Trash bags
- Latex or rubber gloves
- Scrubbing cleaner (such as Comet or Soft Scrub)
- Mop (or you can wash floor with rags if you have a small bathroom)
- Old toothbrush (Obviously, you don't use the same toothbrush to clean your teeth and your house.)

Essential kitchen cleaning supplies

- Glass cleaner
- Oven cleaner
- Rags
- Paper towels
- Dustpan
- Bucket
- White vinegar
- Trash can
- Dishwashing liquid
- Old toothbrush
- Disinfectant spray
- Scrubbing cleaner
- Sponge
- Broom
- Mop
- Latex or rubber gloves
- Baking soda
- Trash bags
- Electrostatic dust mop (especially if you have pets)

Basic living-room and bedroom cleaning supplies

- Vacuum with brush attachments, or a regular vacuum and a handheld vacuum
- Electrostatic dusting cloths
- Electrostatic mop, if you have wood floors
- Duster with extended handle

- Trash can
- Glass cleaner
- Trash bags
- Paper towels

Essential computer cleaning supplies

- Can of compressed air
- Rubbing alcohol
- Water
- Battery-powered computer vacuum cleaner
- Cotton swabs
- Lint-free or microfiber cloth
- Old toothbrush

Cleaning cheap

Buying a different cleaner for every job costs a bundle. Here are some cheap alternatives.

Baking soda—good for scrubbing, cleaning, and deodorizing

Some uses:

- Sprinkle baking soda on damp cloth or sponge and scrub sinks, tubs, showers, or tile.
- Put an open box of baking soda in the refrigerator or freezer to eliminate food odors.
- Sprinkle baking soda on the inside bottom of trash cans to eliminate odors.
- Clean fruits and vegetables by sprinkling baking soda on a clean, damp paper towel and scrubbing produce. Rinse with water.
- Scour pots, pans, or sink with a paste made of a little water mixed with 2 tablespoons of baking soda.

White vinegar—good for cleaning, disinfecting, and deodorizing

Some uses:

- Mix ¼ cup vinegar with 1 quart water to wash windows or glass surfaces.
- Add ½ cup vinegar to 1 gallon water to clean floors.
- Pour ½ cup vinegar and ½ cup water into a microwave-safe bowl. Place inside microwave and bring to a boil (takes about one minute). Remove bowl and wipe down microwave.
- Mix 2 cups vinegar with 2 cups warm water. Use solution to clean and disinfect kitchen counters, stovetop, cabinets, appliances, and painted or tiled walls.
- For greasy messes, wipe full-strength vinegar onto spill or splatter. Wait ten minutes, then wipe with a paper towel.

Hydrogen peroxide—great disinfectant and stain remover (Caution: hydrogen peroxide can bleach fabrics and carpets.)

Some uses:

- Pour or spray a little hydrogen peroxide on a rag; wipe down kitchen or bathroom surfaces to disinfect.
- Pour hydrogen peroxide on cutting boards to kill bacteria.
- Fill sink with cold water; add ¼ cup hydrogen peroxide and some salt. Soak vegetables and fruit to remove bacteria and dirt. Rinse with cold water. Pat dry with a paper towel.
- Pour hydrogen peroxide over toothbrushes to kill germs. Rinse toothbrush with clean water. Air dry.

Rubbing alcohol—strong disinfectant, cleans too!

Some uses:

- Mix ½ cup rubbing alcohol with water in 1-quart spray bottle. Use to clean glass surfaces (including eyeglasses).
- Mix 1 cup rubbing alcohol with 1 cup water to wash miniblinds.
- Dip cotton swab into rubbing alcohol to clean computer keyboard.

Bleach—disinfectant (*Note: Bleach is a harsh chemical. Never use full-strength bleach to clean surfaces. Always wear latex or rubber gloves when cleaning with bleach. Use only in well-ventilated areas, and do not store bleach solutions or mix bleach with any other compounds.*)

Some uses:

- To kill mold and mildew, wipe down surface with a solution of ¼ to ½ cup of bleach and 1 gallon water.
- Pour 1 cup bleach into toilet bowl. Scrub bowl with toilet brush. Wait ten minutes before flushing toilet.
- To sanitize trash cans and diaper pails, wipe down with a solution of ¼ cup bleach and 1 gallon water.

Where does all the dirt come from?

Most of the dirt in your house is tracked in by shoes, feet, or paws. Putting doormats both inside and outside of any exterior doors helps keep dirt from coming inside. Doormats with lots of bristles most efficiently remove dirt. I recommend mats made with AstroTurf, at least for outside use.

Chapter 50

How to Clean

You've got the supplies, and you know what to clean—but *how* do you clean?

General rules of cleaning

- Clean from top to bottom.
- Clean from driest to wettest.
- Clean from cleanest or messiest.
- Clean messes now, not later.
- Clean something every day.

Cleaning the bathroom

Some cleaning needs to happen in the bathroom every day. Make it part of your routine.

Every day

- Use a squeegee to remove water from the shower door and walls before you step out of the shower. This helps prevent soap scum and hard water buildup, mold, and mildew.
- Spray glass cleaner on mirrors and faucets. Dry with a paper towel.
- Use a disinfectant wipe to wipe down counters, sink, and toilet seat—in that order! Or you can spray these surfaces with glass cleaner and wipe down with paper towels.

Tip

Store your bathroom cleaning supplies in one plastic bucket or caddy under the sink for easy reach. It'll make cleaning easier and faster, especially if you have more than one bathroom—you can easily carry supplies from one bathroom to another.

Every other day

- Put bath towels, wash cloths, and hand towels in laundry basket or hamper.
- Put out clean towels.

Every week

- Wipe down any furniture, cabinets, or decorative items with a damp paper towel.
- Pull hair from brushes and combs, then soak brushes and combs in a sink partially filled with warm water and 1 teaspoon of baking soda for thirty minutes. Rinse and air-dry on a towel.
- Use duster or vacuum to remove any dust or spiderwebs from ceiling or blinds.

- Pick up rugs and sweep or vacuum floors.
- Spray tub-and-tile cleaner on ceramic tiles, and scrub clean with a cloth rag or sponge.
- Spray tub-and-tile cleaner on shower or bathtub, and scrub clean with a rag or sponge.
- Spray disinfectant on toilet surfaces, and wipe down entire toilet with clean rag or paper towel. (Don't forget under the rim and around the base of the toilet.)
- Squirt or pour scrubbing cleaner into the toilet bowl, and scrub with a toilet brush. Be sure to use a brush to scrub under the lip, where the water comes out.
- Partially fill sink or bucket with warm water. Add ¼ cup vinegar or disinfectant cleaner. Dampen rag or mop with cleaning solution. Mop tile or linoleum floors.
- Dry floors with a clean rag or paper towel. Use the same towel to wipe down baseboards.
- Empty the trash can. Spray the inside with disinfectant spray and wipe down with a paper towel.
- Put away all cleaners. Put rags with dirty laundry. Rinse out the sponge with warm water and squeeze dry. Put all trash in a trash bag, then remove it from the bathroom.

Every two to three weeks

- Launder bathroom rugs.

Once a year

- Go through medicine cabinet and first-aid kit; discard all expired medications and replace with new ones.

Cleaning the kitchen

Every day

- Wash dishes, or scrape dishes and place them in the dishwasher after every meal. (If you can't wash dishes right away, let them soak in a sink full of warm, soapy water until you can get to them later in the day.)
- Spray glass or surface cleaner on stove top and wipe down after every use.
- Partially fill the sink with clean water and a few drops of liquid dish soap. Wipe down countertops with a soapy rag (or disinfectant cloth) after every use. Wipe down table with soapy rag after every use. Empty sink of soapy water, and wipe down sink with sponge or paper towel after every meal.
- Sweep or vacuum floor.
- Take out trash (as needed—just remember, any food in the trash will spoil and smell up your kitchen, so don't wait a week to empty the trash can).

> **Different rags for different rooms**
>
> Keep separate rags and sponges for bathroom and kitchen cleaning to prevent germs from your bathroom getting into your kitchen and vice versa.

Every week

- Inspect refrigerator contents, and throw out any old food.
- Take out and wash any removable glass plates from the microwave.
- Spray the inside of the microwave with glass or surface cleaner and wipe clean.

- Spray the inside of the trash can with disinfectant spray and wipe clean.
- Fill a bucket or sink with warm water and ½ cup vinegar. Dampen a rag with cleaning solution and wipe down cabinets, the wall behind the stove, switch plates, and refrigerator and microwave doors.
- If your cleaning solution isn't too dirty, use it to mop the floor. If the solution is dirty, make clean solution. If the floor is really damp after mopping, especially if you have a hardwood floor, dry with a cloth rag.
- Wipe switch plates, doorknobs, and telephone with disinfectant wipe.

Every three months or so

- Manual-cleaning oven: clean the inside of the oven with oven cleaner—be sure to follow manufacturer's directions. Always wear latex or rubber gloves when using oven cleaner. Self-cleaning oven: follow manufacturer's directions for how to run the cleaning cycle. After the cycle is completed and the oven has cooled down, wipe away any ash or debris with a damp cloth.
- Clean the refrigerator. Empty out the entire fridge. Fill the sink with warm, soapy water. Pull out any removable shelves and bins from the fridge, and wash them in the sink. Rinse with clean water, and dry with a clean towel. Dampen a rag with soapy water, and wipe down the inside of the refrigerator. Wipe dry with a towel. Put shelves, bins, and food back in the fridge.
- Wipe down walls and baseboards with a damp cloth.

Cleaning the living room

Every day

- Put CDs, DVDs, video games, etc., in their cases and put them away.
- Pick up any trash, old papers, and magazines and throw them away.
- Wipe up any spills.
- Vacuum up any crumbs (a handheld vacuum comes in handy for this small job).
- Straighten any pillows, cushions, or throws.

Every week

- Dust from ceiling to floor using a duster with an extended handle. Remember to dust ceiling fans and miniblinds.
- Dust all furniture, books, electronics (TV, stereo, etc.), and decorative items with a dusting cloth.
- Vacuum cloth or leather furniture. Pick up any cushions and vacuum underneath them.
- Pick up any small area rugs or doormats. Take them outside and shake out the dirt. Vacuum larger area rugs.
- Use vacuum brush attachment to clean lamp shades, windowsills, and heating vents.
- Vacuum the floor. For hardwood floors, vacuum weekly, and damp-mop with warm water every other week.
- Put rugs back down.
- Wipe down switch plates, doorknobs, and telephone with a disinfectant wipe.

Every three months

- Move heavy furniture and vacuum underneath it.
- Vacuum drapes.

Cleaning the bedroom

Every day

- Make the bed.
- Put all dirty clothes in a laundry bag or basket.
- Put away all clean clothes neatly.
- Put CDs, DVDs, video games, etc., in their cases and put them away.
- Pick up any trash, old papers, and magazines and throw them away.
- Wipe up any spills.
- Vacuum up any crumbs (a handheld vacuum comes in handy for this small job).

Every week

- Strip the bed, put dirty sheets in the laundry, and make up the bed with clean sheets.
- Dust from ceiling to floor using a duster with an extended handle. Remember to dust ceiling fans and miniblinds.
- Dust all furniture, books, electronics (TV, stereo, etc.), and decorative items with a dusting cloth.
- Pick up any small area rugs. Take them outside and shake out the dirt. Vacuum larger area rugs.

- Use vacuum brush attachment to clean lamp shades, windowsills, and heating vents.
- Vacuum the floor. For hardwood floors, vacuum weekly, and damp-mop with warm water every other week.
- Put rugs back down.
- Wipe down switch plates, doorknobs, and telephone with a disinfectant wipe.

Every three months

- Vacuum, rotate, and turn over mattress.
- Vacuum under all heavy furniture.
- Vacuum drapes.

Once a year

- Clean and straighten all closets.

Cleaning the computer/office area

Every day

- Go through mail. Throw away the junk.
- Place all bills in a file folder or basket.
- Write down any new events or appointments in a planner or calendar.
- File any loose papers. Throw away what you don't need.
- Pick everything up off the floor and put it away.
- Tidy the desk.
- Enter any purchases in your checkbook. File receipts for tax purposes.

Zapping your computer

Static electricity can fry components of your computer. For this reason, it's wise to always turn off your computer while you're cleaning the computer or around it. Also, never use an electric vacuum to clean your computer.

Every week

- Pay bills, then file billing statements.
- Make sure your checkbook is up to date.
- Look at your planning calendar for that week. Make any changes.
- Turn off your computer, then dust furniture surfaces and sweep or vacuum floors.
- With computer off, use clean, dry, microfiber cloth to dust the computer monitor.
- With computer off, wipe keyboard keys with a cotton swab dipped in rubbing alcohol. (Swab should be damp, not dripping.)

Every three months

- Turn off computer.
- Disconnect the keyboard from the computer. Hold the keyboard upside down over the trash can and shake gently to remove any crumbs and dirt. Turn keyboard right side up and use compressed air to clean out any remaining dust. Wipe down keyboard keys with a cotton swab dipped in rubbing alcohol. (Swab should be damp, not dripping)

- Disconnect the mouse. Turn mouse upside down and clean out dirt with compressed air. Wipe the top and bottom of the mouse with a cotton swab dipped in rubbing alcohol (again, damp, not dripping).
- Use battery-powered computer vacuum cleaner to vacuum dust and dirt on the outside of the monitor and case.
- Dampen clean microfiber cloth with water. Wipe down monitor screen.

Outdoor chores

Every day

- Pick up any litter.

Every week

- Shake out all doormats.
- Use a broom to sweep away any spiderwebs.
- Sweep patios, decks, porches, and garage.
- Remove trash from your car and vacuum the car's interior.
- Wash the car, if necessary.
- Take out trash to be collected.

Seasonal

- Rake leaves.
- Shovel snow and remove ice.
- Mow the lawn.
- Maintain landscaping.

Chapter 51

A Routine to Stay Clean

Fifteen minutes a day. Yes, just fifteen minutes a day in addition to your daily chores will keep your house clean. There are exceptions, like the day after hosting a Super Bowl party or when doing heavy-duty cleaning. But for normal, everyday life, fifteen minutes of cleaning each day will make your house sparkle.

Start with everyday chores (see previous chapter for detailed list). Every day, you . . .

- make your bed.
- wipe down kitchen and bathroom surfaces.
- wash dishes.
- pick up anything on the floor.
- put things where they belong.

- put trash in the trash can.
- clean up any messes.

Next, look at the chores you need to do weekly, and plan which day you're going to do them. Your cleaning plan will depend on your schedule. You may have days when you just can't do more than the daily cleaning chores, so you'll have to double up on another day.

Laundry will take more than fifteen minutes (more like a couple of hours), but you do need to fit it into your schedule.

Focus on one room a day for fifteen minutes. For example:

Monday	Tuesday	Wednesday	Thursday	Friday	Saturday	Sunday
Clean living room	Clean office area	Do outside chores	Clean kitchen	Clean bathroom	Do laundry	Rest

Making it happen

- Make a cleaning plan that fits your schedule.
- Write down the plan on your planner or calendar. Mark specific dates for specific chores.
- Look at the planner or calendar every day.
- Just do it!

Now look at the chores that have to be done less frequently, and plan which month you'll do those chores. For example:

January—Clean inside oven, and clean refrigerator.

February—Move heavy furniture in living room and bedroom and vacuum; vacuum drapes; rotate mattress.

March—Clean computer.

April—Clean inside oven, and clean refrigerator.

May—Wash windows inside and out.

June—Landscaping, clean garage.

July—Clean inside oven, and clean refrigerator.

August—Move heavy furniture in living room and bedroom and vacuum; vacuum drapes; rotate mattress.

September—Clean computer.

October—Clean inside oven, and clean refrigerator.

November—Move heavy furniture in living room and bedroom and vacuum; vacuum drapes; rotate mattress.

December—Clean and straighten closets; inspect medicine cabinet and first-aid kit, discarding anything expired and replacing with new items.

Does a call from your mom telling you she's on her way to visit cause you to hyperventilate because of the state of your living quarters? Developing and maintaining a cleaning routine will help you to not become overwhelmed with too much cleaning at one time, and it also will allow you to entertain family and friends without going into panic mode.

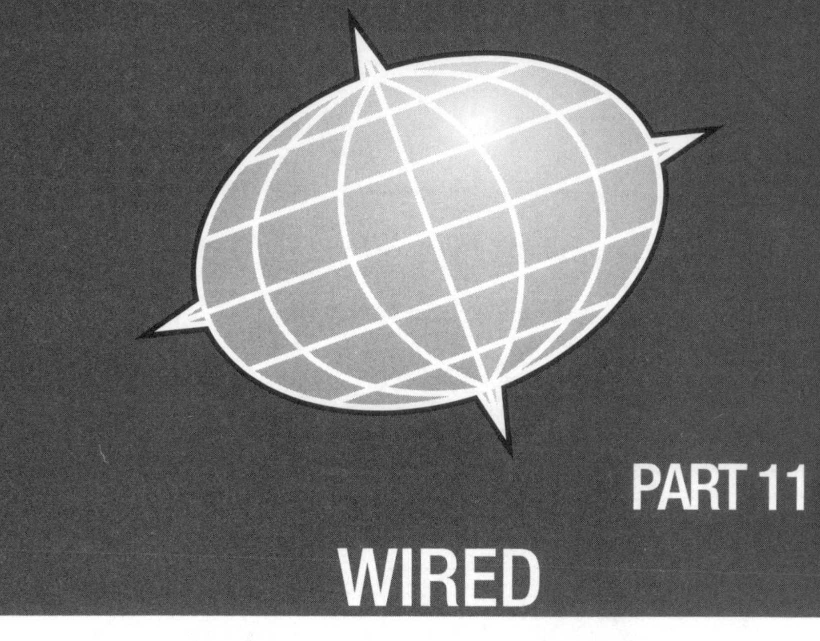

PART 11

WIRED

Where do you shop? Where do you get your news? How do you communicate with others? Where do you search for information? Where do you work? Where do you keep track of finances? Where do you get your entertainment?

More than likely, you do some, if not all, of these things via computer and the Internet. Studies show that young adults spend an average of 16.7 hours online each week.[21] If that's the case, you'll spend more than five years of your adulthood on the Web. It's almost like you live there.

Living anyplace requires knowing your way around, being aware of dangers, and knowing how to stay safe. The following chapters provide a map for safely navigating the Internet and avoiding its pitfalls.

Chapter 52

Spiders on the Web

They say the Internet is a dangerous place.

You laugh in the face of danger.

After all, you know your way around the World Wide Web much better than your parents ever will. It's a tough neighborhood, but you can handle it. Right?

Yet according to the National Consumers League (NCL), 25 percent of the victims of Internet fraud in 2006 were between the ages of twenty and twenty-nine.[22]

In 2005, 29 percent of all identity thefts happened to people eighteen to twenty-nine years old.[23]

And about one third of you have already had a "scary" experience online.[24]

So what to do? Simple. Know what the dangers look like and avoid them like the plague. Here are some of the dangers lurking on the Net:

People wanting to hurt somebody

"Federal authorities believe that at least 500,000 to 750,000 predators are 'online' on a daily basis," according to Clint Van Zandt of MSNBC.com.[25]

People (hackers) and viruses that can hurt your computer

As of January 2006, 185,000 computer viruses existed, and the number grows daily.[26] A computer hacker strikes every 39 seconds, according to a University of Maryland study.[27]

People trying to take your money (fraud)

More than 79,000 people reported losing money through Internet scams in 2006, according to the FBI.[28]

People wanting to be you (identity theft)

Every minute in 2006, 28.5 people became new victims of identity theft in the United States, according to Identity Theft Resource Center.[29]

People engaging in immoral and/or illegal behavior

Gambling

"Statistics prove that teenage Internet gambling is the fastest growing addiction of the day, akin to drug and alcohol abuse in the

1930s," said David Robertson, former chairman of the National Coalition Against Legalized Gambling.[30]

Pornography

"Two in five Internet users visited an adult site in August of 2005, according to tracking by comScore Media Metrix."[31]

Theft

According to the Barna Group, "Overall, 4 out of every 5 teenagers (80%) have engaged in some type of music piracy in the past six months—including making copies of CDs for other people, downloading free music (other than promotions or giveaways), or uploading their own music files to the Internet to share with others."[32]

Chapter 53

Playing It Safe on the Web

Now that you know what the dangers are, here are some Internet safety tips.

To avoid contact with a predator

- Do not communicate with strangers online.
- Do not share your name, address, age, phone number, birthday, e-mail address, Social Security number, or the name of your workplace or school online.
- Do not send a photo of yourself to anyone you haven't met in person.
- Do not post pictures of yourself online for the whole world to see. Use only secure online photo albums that require a password to view.

- Do not post your schedule or activities online. (Example: "Going to Starbucks this Friday night" or, "I play volleyball with the Tigers.")
- Save any threatening messages with the time and date you received them.
- Contact the police if you receive any threatening e-mails, postings, or Instant Messages (IMs) or if you feel threatened in any way.
- Never, ever, meet with someone in person that you met online.
- Do not reply to an IM or e-mail from somebody you don't know.

To avoid damage to your computer

- Don't open attachments sent to you from someone you don't know.
- Run antivirus software, and update it often.
- Run a spyware protection program such as Ad-Aware or Spybot. Keep this program updated.
- Enable your computer's firewall.
- Do not visit warez sites.
- Run an online virus scan every three months or so.
- Avoid free software offers that you have not researched. Many of these will download spyware onto your computer.
- Create strong passwords (see next chapter), and change them often.

To avoid identity theft or being scammed

- Do not reply to an e-mail from someone you don't know.
- Always check out company information before responding to an offer by searching for the company on the Internet or checking with the Better Business Bureau.
- Never give personal information via e-mail, such as bank account numbers, Social Security number, birth date, passwords, or credit card numbers.
- Never respond to an e-mail that looks like it comes from your bank, credit card company, or another company with which you have an account.

Some popular spyware removers

- Ad-Aware (www.lavasoft.com)
- Spybot (www.spybot.info)
- Spyblaster (www.spyblaster.com)

Some popular antivirus programs

- BitDefender (www.bitdefender.com)
- McAfee Virus Scan (www.mcafee.com)
- Avast! Antivirus (www.avast.com)

- Do not click on Web-site links in e-mails that look like they are from a company. Always open a new Internet browser screen and type in the company's correct URL yourself.
- Use antivirus and antispyware software as well as a firewall on your computer. Update them regularly.
- If something looks too good to be true, go to www.snopes.com and check it out.
- Know that wealthy foreigners do not need your help moving their assets out of their country.

To avoid immoral or illegal activity

- Be active in things that are good and right.
- Know where you stand on moral issues and why.
- Do not visit pornographic Web sites.
- Do not visit gambling or gaming Web sites.
- Do not visit warez sites.
- Do not download pirated music, software, movies, or other products.
- Install filtering software on your computer.
- Have an accountability partner that has access to your online activity, including e-mails.

Don't get hooked by phishing

Phishing is when a criminal sends you an e-mail that looks like it comes from a real business, such as your bank, Internet service provider, or online auction site. The e-mail usually claims that you need to update your account information right away or your account will expire. You will be asked to reply immediately and to send personal information, such as your account numbers, passwords, or Social Security number.

Once you send your personal information, the bad guys use it to steal your identity, run up your credit card bills, or commit crimes in your name.

If you believed you've been phished, you can report it by sending e-mail to phishing-report@us-cert.gov. Visit www.consumer.gov/idtheft for more information.

What is warez?

Warez is the name Internet pirates use for copyrighted material that is made available to download illegally via the Internet.

Some popular accountability/filter software

- X3watch (www.x3watch.com)
- Covenant Eyes (www.covenanteyes.com)
- ChatChecker (www.chatchecker.com)

Chapter 54

Passwords

A lot of Web sites require you to register a username and password. To protect your privacy, usernames should be something other than your real name. Creating a password difficult for hackers to crack protects you and your computer.

Tips for creating a strong password

- Use at least twelve characters. The more characters, the better.
- Use a combination of lowercase letters, uppercase letters, numbers, and symbols when possible.
- Don't use words found in any dictionary of any language.
- Don't use your name, pet's name, address, birth date, or other personal information.

- Don't use your username as your password.
- Avoid repeating the same letter or number (example: TTTT).
- Don't use the same password on every Internet account.
- Change your password at least three times a year.
- Don't keep your password where other people can find it (like on a piece of paper).

How to create a strong password

The key to creating a good password is making it easy for you to remember and difficult for others to find out. Here are some steps to help you do that.

1. Start with a complete sentence or phrase, using lower- and uppercase letters: My Cat Lucy Had Eight Kittens.
2. Take the first two letters of each word: MyCaLuHaEiKi
3. Replace some of the letters with numbers: MyC4L0Ha8K1
4. Replace some letters with symbols, or add some symbols: !MyC4L0H&8K1!
5. Write out your new password five to ten times.
6. Try to write your password down by memory. If you can't do it, repeat step 5 until you can.
7. Log into your account using your new password without looking at your paper. Log out. Do it again.
8. After you've memorized your password, destroy the paper you wrote it on.

Chapter 55

Techno Lingo

Communicating efficiently via e-mail, message boards, IMs, and text messages requires typing what you need to say with the fewest keystrokes possible. A new "language" has emerged out of this need for brevity and clarity on the Web.

Essential dictionary of Web words

2B | ^2B...... To be or not to be

411....................... Information

@TEOTD .... At the end of the day

AAF .... As a friend

AAR..................... At any rate

404....................... I don't know

?4U .... Question for you

2NITE .... Tonight

AAK......... Asleep at keyboard

AAYF .. As always, your friend

ADD............................ Address

ABT2 .... About to
ADN .... Any Day Now
AFAIK ....As far as I know
AKA................Also known as
AML.....................All my love
ASAP.......As soon as possible
AYEC ....At your earliest convenience
B .... Be
BBIAB........... Be back in a bit
B4 .... Before
B4U .... Before you
BBIAF .... Be back in a few
BCNU ....Be seeing you
BFF ....Best friends forever
BM&Y... Between me and you
BRB .... Be right back
BTDT.. Been there, done that
CMIIW ....Correct me if I'm wrong
CR8 ....Create
C-T..................................City
CUL .... See you later
DCC (Direct Client to Client).............Start a chat
D/L .... Download
AEAP.......As early as possible
AISB .... As it should be
ALOL.........Actually laughing out loud
AOTA .... All of the above
ATM............. At the moment
AYOR.......... At your own risk
BB.................... Bulletin board
B/C ....Because
B4N .... Bye for now
BAK ...... Back at my keyboard
BBL ....Be back later
BF .... Best friend
BIF.....................Before I forget
BOX .... Computer
BTA.................But then again
BTW ....By the way
CMON ....Come on
CSL ....Can't stop laughing
CU............................. See you
CY .... Calm yourself
DEGT....................Don't even go there
DQMOT .... Don't quote me on this
EAK......... Eating at keyboard

DTS................ Don't think so
EBKAC .... Error between keyboard and chair
EMA................ E-mail address
EOM.............. End of message
EZ .... Easy
F2T .... Free to talk
FTTB......... For the time being
FYEO......... For your eyes only
G .... Grin
GA .... Go ahead
GBH................ Great big hug
GFI .... Go for it
GIGO...... Garbage in, garbage out
GOI .... Get over it
GT .... Good try
H&K .... Hugs and kisses
H8 .... Hate
HB .... Hurry back
HF .... Have fun
HRU................. How are you?
I 1-D-R .... I wonder
IB.............................. I'm back
IDK.................... I don't know
IDTS .... I don't think so
EM........................ Excuse me?
EOD .... End of day
ERR .... Getting mad
F2F........................ Face to face
FBM...................... Fine by me
FWIW ...... For what it's worth
FYI......... For your information
G2R...................... Got to run
GB .... Good-bye
GBU .... God bless you
GIAR .... Give it a rest
GMTA ...... Great minds think alike
GR8............................... Great
GTG....................... Got to go
H2CUS Hope to see you soon
HAGO .... Have a good one
HD................................. Hold
HHOJ .... Ha-ha, only joking
HTH............. Hope this helps
IAC .... In any case
IC .... I see
IDST .... I didn't say that
IIRC .. If I remember correctly
IK................................ I know
ILU .... I love you

IM................... Instant message
IMO...................In my opinion
IOH...................I'm outta here
IRMC................ I rest my case
IYKWIM .. If you know what I mean
J/T .... Just teasing
JK.......................... Just kidding
KBD.......................... Keyboard
KIT...................Keep in touch
L8R................................ Later
LOL........... Laughing out loud
MOOS............Member of the opposite sex
MSG.......................... Message
NOOB........................ Newbie
N2M.............. Not to mention
NE .... Anyway
NFM.................. None for me
NM....................... Never mind
NP .... No problem
NW .... No way
OOC .... Out of control
OOTD........ One of these days
OTL...................Out to lunch
PCM................ Please call me
IMHO In my humble opinion
IMS ....I'm sorry
IRL .... In real life
IUSS.................... If you say so
J/C ....Just chillin' or just checking
JAM................... Just a minute
K ....Okay
KIR.......................Keep it real
KWIM .....Know what I mean?
LMK ....Let me know
LTNS........... Long time no see
MOSS ....Member of the same sex
MTF ....More to follow
N1 ....Nice one
NBD .... No big deal
NE1 ....Anyone
NLT ....No later than
NMP............ Not my problem
NTK ....Nice to know
OBTW .... Oh, by the way
OOH .... Out of here
OT............................ Off topic
OTT ....Over the top
PLMK.......Please let me know

PIC .... Picture
PMFI .... Pardon me for interrupting
POOF .... Good-bye
PTL .... Praise the Lord
PU .... That stinks
P-ZA .... Pizza
QIK .... Quick
RBAY .... Right back at you
RL .... Real life
RN .... Right now
RTM .... Read the manual
SC .... Stay cool
SETE .... Smiling ear-to-ear
SIT .... Stay in touch
SMAIM... Send me an instant message
SMHID ... Scratching my head in disbelief
SS .... So sorry
STW .... Search the Web
SYL .... See you later
TA .... Thanks a lot
TBC .... To be continued
TBH .... To be honest
TFN .... Thanks for nothing
TIC .... Tongue in cheek
PM .... Private message
POAHF ... Put on a happy face
PPL .... People
PTMM ..... Please tell me more
PXT .... Please explain that
Q .... Queue
QT .... Cutie
RBTL Read between the lines
RME .... Rolling my eyes
ROFL .... Rolling on the floor laughing
RUOK .... Are you okay?
SCNR... Sorry, could not resist
SFX .... Sound effects
SLAP .... Sounds like a plan
SMEM ...... Send me an e-mail
SO .... Significant other
SPK .... Speak
SRY .... Sorry
SSINF So stupid it's not funny
SUP .... What's up?
T+ .... Think positive
TAFN .... That's all for now
TBD .... To be determined
TC .... Take care
THX .... Thanks
TM .... Trust me

TMI .... Too much information
TOM .... Tomorrow
TSTB... The sooner the better
TTG .... Time to go
TYT .... Take your time
U2 .... You too?
UL .... Upload
UW .... You're welcome
VBG .... Very big grin
VSF .... Very sad face
W/E .... Whatever
WAI.................. What an idiot
WBU .... What about you?
WDYT.... What do you think?
WK................................ Week
WOMBAT ... Waste of money, brains, and time
WYS........... Whatever you say
X .... Kiss
XME .... Excuse me
YGBKYou've got to be kidding
YKW .... You know what?
YYSSW .... Yeah, yeah, sure, sure, whatever
TMOT.......... Trust me on this
TPTB....... The powers that be
TTFN .... Ta-ta for now
TTUL........... Talk to you later
U .... You
UGTBK.........You've got to be kidding
VM .... Voice mail
W/B .... Write back
W/O .... Without
WAM .... Wait a minute
WDYS .... What did you say?
WFM .... Works for me
WKD .... Weekend
WRUD.. What are you doing?
WTG...................... Way to go
WYP.....What's your problem?
WYWH ... Wish you were here
XLNT........................ Excellent
YA .... Yet another
YHM .... You have mail
YNK ....You never know
ZZZ................................ Bored

Essential emoticon list

#:-o ....Shocked
%-) .... Silly
%-{................................Ironic
>:-< .... Angry
>=^P...............................Yuck
(()):** ....Hugs and kisses
^^^ .... Laughter
8-O .... Astonished
;) .... Smile
:() ....Loudmouth
:-# ....My lips are sealed
:-p ....Sticking out tongue
:@................................What?!
:-x ....My lips are sealed, or sealed with a kiss
:{ .... Having a hard time
%-(.......................... Confused
-6%........................Brain-dead
>;-(...........................Annoyed
>>:-<<.........................Furious
<;-) ...Innocently asking dumb question
(:-\ .... Very sad
0;-)................................Angel
8-[.................................Wow!
: | .... Bored
:,(.................................Crying
:-e .... Disappointed
:-O ....Surprised
:-V ....Shouting
;/)...........................Not funny
':-)..................Raised eyebrow

PART 12
ACTIVE CITIZENSHIP

The day you turned eighteen, *poof!* Something magical happened, at least in the eyes of our legal system. In the United States, at age eighteen you are an official, legitimate adult citizen, with all the rights and responsibilities.

As an adult you can

- sign binding contracts.
- buy or sell property, including real estate and stocks.
- marry (without the permission of a parent).
- sue or be sued.
- make or revoke a will.
- inherit property outright (without it going into a trust).
- vote.

- consent to all types of medical treatment.
- join the military (without the permission of a parent).
- serve on a jury.
- face much more serious consequences for breaking the law.
- buy some types of guns.

Your responsibilities include

- making a positive impact on society.
- protecting the innocent (especially children and the elderly).
- being an active member in a faith community.
- engaging in community affairs.
- educating yourself regarding political issues, candidates, and where the candidates stand on the issues.
- voting intelligently.
- reporting any illegal activity to the proper authorities.
- if male, registering for selective service.

In this section, we'll look at the new ways you, as an adult, can make an impact and make the world a better place.

Chapter 56

Registering to Vote

Your vote does make a difference. Two votes decided a New Hampshire race for the Senate. One vote made all the difference in a 2004 Salt Lake City school board election. And the winner of a 2004 Montana House of Representatives seat won by two votes.

The strength of the United States democratic system depends on every eligible voter going to the polls on Election Day.

When do I register to vote?

Anytime after you turn 17½ years old, but before the voter registration deadline in your state. For most states, the deadline is about thirty days before an election. You must be eighteen years old on or before the election in order to vote.

Where do I register to vote?

- At your state's Department of Motor Vehicles (DMV) offices when you apply for or renew your driver's license
- Online at www.fec.gov, www.vote411.org, or www.registervote.com
- At local election offices
- At military recruitment offices

What next?

- You should receive a voter identification card when you register or in the mail shortly thereafter.
- Bring the voter ID card, along with your driver's license or other form of photo ID when you go to vote.

Chapter 57

Making Your Mark

When to vote

Federal elections are always held on the Tuesday after the first Monday in November. State and local governments usually hold their general elections on the same day. Governments may call a special election on a different day in the case of a tied vote, a death or removal from office of an elected official, or legislation requiring immediate action.

Most states require employers to allow workers to leave work in order to vote if the employees' work schedule does not allow enough time to vote before or after work.

When polling places open and close varies by state. Most polling places open between 7–8:00 A.M. and close between

7–9:00 P.M. To find specific information for your state, go to http://www.eac.gov/docs/poll%20hours%20survey.pdf.

Where to vote

Your home address determines at which polling place you vote. To find your polling place, visit www.canivote.org or contact your state election office. Your polling place should also be printed on your voter registration card.

What to bring

Most states require that you show some photo identification at the polling place before you can vote. A current driver's license will usually do the trick. To check your state's ID requirements, visit www.canivote.org or contact your state's election office.

How to vote

Study a sample ballot before you enter the voting booth. Find sample ballots for upcoming elections in your local newspaper or through the League of Women Voters, www.lwv.org and search for "sample ballots." You can also Google your town name, state, and sample ballot. Read chapter 58 to learn how to educate yourself about the candidates and legislation on your ballot.

When you're out of town on Election Day

When you know work, travel, or health issues will prevent you from going to your local polling place on Election Day, vote using an absentee ballot. Contact your state election office to request an absentee ballot. Or visit a political party's Web site, such as www.gop.com/voteearly/ or https://electionimpact.votenet.com/dnc/voterreg/index.cfm and request that an absentee ballot be sent to you. For information regarding absentee voting when you're out of the country, go to http://travel.state.gov/law/info/info_2964.html.

Problem at the poll

What if you get to your polling place and the election officials say you're not registered to vote or you're at the wrong polling place? Ask for a provisional ballot. A provisional ballot allows you to go ahead and vote, and it allows time for election officials to verify your voter registration and the location where your ballot should be cast.

Chapter 58

What You'll Vote For

Are you for or against? How can you know for whom or for what to vote?

What's on the ballot

Candidates running for local, state, and federal offices

Voters elect more than just the president! You could be voting for . . .

- Judges
- City commissioner
- City council members
- State representatives
- Sheriff
- District attorney
- Mayor
- State treasurer

- Secretary of state
- Lieutenant governor
- County administrator
- Trustees
- U.S. representative
- Governor
- Attorney general
- County recorder
- U.S. senator

Sources for voting guides

- Christian Coalition of America (www.cc.org/voterguides.cfm)
- Smart Voter (www.smartvoter.org)
- Values Voters (www.valuesvoters.com)

Initiatives

In some states voters have the right to gather enough signatures on a petition to force a public vote on an issue like an ordinance, change, or addition to the state constitution, or charter amendment.

Referendums

A referendum is a public vote to overturn legislation already passed by state officials.

Tax levies

A tax levy is a bill proposing to alter (usually raise) property taxes for a particular tax-funded institution, such as schools, fire stations, or senior services.

Propositions

Each proposition is a bill that requires a public vote in order to become law.

Tips for becoming a smart voter

- Study voting guides (made available by various organizations).
- Study sample ballots before you vote.
- Visit candidates' Web sites and read what they have to say about themselves.
- Go to www.votesmart.org and look at a candidate's previous voting record, biography, and where he or she stands on various issues.

Understanding tax levy

Tax levies usually raise the amount of property tax a person has to pay in order to finance a tax-funded operation, such as a school, hospital, or library. Levies cover day-to-day operating expenses, or they may be for a certain project, like a new fire department. Tax levies can also reduce or cut funding. Most levies expire after a certain amount of time.

So let's say you own a house worth $100,000 according to your local tax assessor. The school district places a levy on the ballot to raise money for a new elementary school. The school levy for 2 mil passes. (By the way, a mil rate is the dollar amount per $1,000 of assessed tax value of your property, and 1 mil = $.001.)

You can figure out the impact of a levy on your property tax bill:

- Market value x assessment ratio (determined by your county) = assessed valuation.
- Assessed valuation x mil levy = cost to you.

So, if you owned a house worth $100,000 and the assessment ratio for your county is 50 percent:

- 100,000 x .50 = $50,000 (your assessed valuation)
- $50,000 x 2 mil (.002) = $100 per year increase in your property tax bill.

Chapter 59

You? Run for Office?

Want to make a difference in your city, state, or country? Why not run for political office? You can, you know. At the age of eighteen, you became eligible to run for almost any public office except for the Senate (you need to be thirty) and president of the United States (you have to be almost ancient—thirty-five!)

What you can be

Check with your state election office for specific age, residence, and experience requirements for the office that interests you. Here are some options:

- School board member
- Trustee
- Sheriff
- Village/township clerk
- Auditor
- City commissioner

- District attorney
- Mayor
- State treasurer
- Governor
- Attorney general
- County recorder
- City council member
- State representative
- Secretary of state
- Lieutenant governor
- County administrator

Running for Office in Six Steps

1. Choose the office, and make sure you meet the qualification requirements.
2. Choose a party. Some offices are nonpartisan, but most will require you to register as a member of a political party (Republican, Democrat, Libertarian, etc.).
3. Collect signatures required in order for you to be nominated.
4. File your nomination with state election officials.
5. Get organized and campaign.
6. Vote on Election Day.

Chapter 60

Active in Your Community

Running for office isn't the only way to serve your community. Volunteering makes the impossible possible. Coming alongside someone whose home has been destroyed or a child who can't read and lending them a hand has a positive impact on everyone. Today's technology allows you to find the perfect volunteer opportunity. You can even volunteer without leaving home!

Good reasons to volunteer

- Change someone's life for the better.
- Show God's love by serving others.
- Acquire new skills.
- Build your resume.
- Expand your world.

- Form new friendships.
- Build connections with your community.
- Make life more interesting and rewarding.
- Feel good about something you've done.

Ways to search for volunteer opportunities

- ***By faith***—Volunteer at your church or another faith-based organization.
- ***By community***—If you want to stay close to home, look for opportunities to serve within your neighborhood. Want to see the world? Hook up with a global volunteer organization.
- ***By skill***—Are you really good at something? Or is there something you'd like to learn how to do? Look for an opportunity to share or learn a particular skill.
- ***By passion***—Have you always wanted to help poor, orphaned children? Do political campaigns excite you? Are you into preserving nature? Link up with an organization that shares your passion.
- ***By opportunity***—Looking for the chance to travel? Would you like to attend theater performances? Volunteer at places that provide you specific opportunities.

How to find the right place to serve

- Look at Web sites devoted to matching volunteers with service opportunities. (See "Meet your match" at the end of this chapter.)
- Ask your pastor about volunteer opportunities in the community as well as in the church.

- Talk to other people who volunteer.
- Research organizations with which you might be interested in volunteering.

Volunteering with benefits

- Learn how to save a life when volunteering for organizations like the Red Cross, Citizen Corps, or other emergency services organizations.
- See concerts or theater performances free when you volunteer as an usher at a local performing-arts center.
- Free admission to zoos, aquariums, and museums when you're an active volunteer.
- Some medical facilities extend free health services to their volunteers.
- Discounts and meal vouchers may be offered.
- Free workshops and training are often made available to volunteers.

Volunteering to serve your country

Joining one of our nation's armed services not only allows you to see the world but to serve your country and its citizens. The military offers some amazing opportunities. Having your education paid for, including medical and graduate school, is just one benefit of military service. Others include complete health-care coverage, thirty days of paid vacation per year, and retirement benefits after twenty years of service. Contact your local recruiter or visit the following Web sites for more information.

- **Air Force** www.airforce.com
- **Army** www.goarmy.com

- **Coast Guard** www.gocoastguard.com
- **Marines** www.marines.com
- **National Guard** www.ngb.army.mil
- **Navy** www.navy.com
- **Peace Corps** www.peacecorps.gov
- **AmeriCorps** www.americorps.gov
- **Teach for America** www.teachforamerica.org

Virtual volunteering

Want to volunteer from home? Tons of opportunities exist without having to travel outside your front door. What can you do from home?

- Web-site design
- Accounting
- Praying
- Writing
- Sewing
- Making phone calls
- Computer programming
- Graphic design
- Fund-raising
- Knitting
- Translating

Meet your match

Below are some Web sites devoted to matching people with volunteer opportunities:

- ChristianVolunteering.org (www.christianvolunteering.org)
- VolunteerMatch (www.volunteermatch.org)
- USA Freedom Corps (www.usafreedomcorps.gov)
- Take Pride in America (www.takepride.gov)

For guys only: register for selective service

The law requires virtually all male U.S. citizens (regardless of where they live), and male immigrants residing in the U.S. (permanent resident aliens), to register within 30 days of their 18th birthday. Therefore, to be in full compliance with the law, a man turning 18 is required to register during the period of time beginning 30 days before, until 30 days after his 18th birthday . . . a 60-day window.

Late registrations are accepted, but not once a man reaches age 26. Men who do not register within the 60-day window are technically in violation of the law and should register as soon as possible.[33] You can register:

- online at www.sss.gov.
- at the post office.
- on a Free Application for Federal Student Aid (FAFSA).
- at a high school.

Chapter 61

Law and Consequences

Breaking the law as an adult has serious consequences, even beyond jail time or fines. Having a criminal record negatively impacts a person's life by limiting many opportunities, including employment, business, education, and housing.

Crime categories

Misdemeanor

A misdemeanor crime carries a maximum jail term of one year and/or a $1,000 fine. Punishment may also include probation and community service. Examples of misdemeanors include shoplifting less then $300 worth of merchandise, criminal trespassing, or disorderly conduct.

Felony

A felony crime carries more than a one-year jail term and a $1,000 fine. Felons permanently lose some civil liberties, such as the right to vote and the right to purchase a gun. Examples of felonies include murder, robbery, rape, possession of child pornography, and vehicular manslaughter.

Felony consequences

Besides jail time and fines, being convicted of a felony crime brings several serious consequences. A convicted felon:

- is not eligible to run for or hold public office.
- is ineligible for seven years to serve on a jury.
- is not permitted to own a gun.
- is not eligible to vote.[34]
- may lose his or her professional license.
- is not eligible to be a foster parent or to adopt a child.
- may be restricted from living in certain areas, depending on the nature of the crime.
- may be evicted from public housing, depending on the nature of the crime.
- may not be eligible for federal student loans or aid.

Jobs not open to felons

- Teacher
- Private detective
- Attorney
- Radiographer
- Architect
- Medical professional
- Judge
- Midwife

- Major contractor
- Psychologist
- Bondsman
- Day-care provider
- Other jobs, based on the nature of the crime
- Public accountant
- Insurance salesperson
- Pawnbroker
- Pharmacist

It's a crime . . .

not to include your criminal record on a job application when asked.

PART 13
IMPORTANT INFORMATION

When you were a child, someone else kept track of all your legal records and documents. In an emergency, someone else contacted family and friends. Now that "someone else" is you. The next few chapters review what you need to have on hand, where to keep it, and why.

Chapter 62

Important Documents

You want to go places, buy stuff, and do things. Many times, doing the grown-up things in life requires certain paperwork. For example:

- To apply for a passport, you need a certified birth certificate or proof of citizenship, a valid driver's license or government ID, plus your Social Security number.
- To apply for a loan, you need copies of your W-2 tax forms, recent pay stubs, bank statements, your Social Security number, and photo ID.

You should keep track of certain documents and records so you'll have them when you need them. (And you will need them!) Here are some important documents you should keep in a lockable box:

- Certified birth certificate or proof of citizenship
- Social Security card
- School transcripts
- Any letters of recommendation, recognition, or award
- All banking documents—statements, account numbers, etc.
- Copy of all contracts—leases, real estate purchases, loan papers, etc.
- Your official will
- Health insurance policy and card
- Health/medical records
- Car insurance policy

Lock 'em up!

Replacing these documents is a major pain, so you'll want to keep them in a safe place. Keep items in a small, lockable, fireproof box and tuck the box out of sight. This is not something you should leave out in the open. However, let a family member or pastor know the location of the box and its contents. In case of an emergency, someone else may need access to your personal information.

Chapter 63

Emergency Contact List

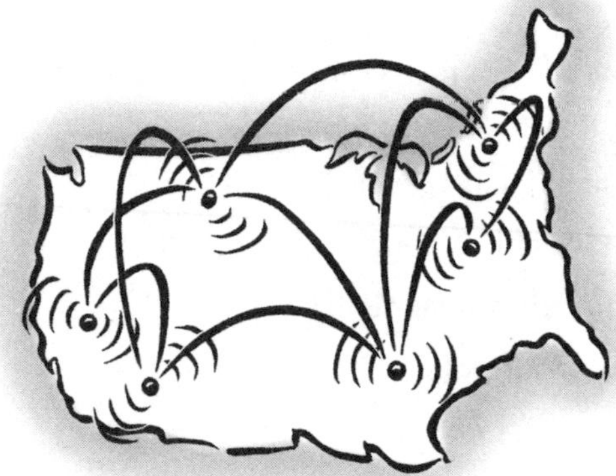

"Mom was rushed to the hospital this morning," my sister said over the phone one evening.

"Why didn't anyone call me?" I asked.

"Nobody had your work or cell phone number."

That was enough for our family to create an emergency contact list with everyone's home, work, and cell phone numbers. Since family members are the first to sense that something isn't right but often live long distances apart, we also gathered contact information of one neighbor or best friend whom family members could contact in case of an extreme emergency.

If something of importance happened in your family, would you know how to get ahold of everyone? Now that you're on your own, would your family be able to contact you?

Who should be on the list

Level 1

- Parents and spouses
- Siblings and spouses

Level 2

- Grandparents
- Aunts
- Uncles

Level 3

- Cousins
- Close family friends

Necessary information

Besides the person's name, address and home phone number, you want to make sure you have the following:

- name of workplace or school.
- work and cell phone numbers.
- their relationship to you.
- an emergency contact not living with that person but near that person (example: neighbor, coworker, best friend).

Below is an example of what your contact list might contain.

Your emergency contact list

Full name ______________________________

Relationship ______________________________

Home phone ________________ Cell phone ________________

Home e-mail ____

Work e-mail ________________ Instant message ID__________

Home address ______________________________________

City ________________ State __________ Zip ____________

Name of workplace/school ____________________________

Work/school phone ___________________________________

Emergency contact name ______________________________

Relationship ____

Home phone ________________ Cell phone ________________

Work phone ________________ Other ____________________

Address ____

Notes ____

Notes

Chapter 4

1. Paul Bannister, "25 Fascinating Facts about Personal Debt," Bankrate.com, September 20, 2004, http://www.bankrate.com/brm/news/debt/debtguide2004/debt-trivia1.asp.

Chapter 15

2. U.S. Department of Housing and Urban Development, "PMI Act Information," www.hud.gov/offices/hsg/sfh/res/respapmi.cfm.

Chapter 19

3. Adapted from "What is a cult?" by Don Veinot, *Campus Life*, July/August 2001, http://www.christianitytoday.com/cl/2001/004/9.43.html.

Chapter 23

4. American Association of Suicidology, "U.S.A. Suicide: 2004 Official Final Data," http://www.suicidology.org/associations/1045/files/2004datapgv1.pdf.

5. Ella Mae Bard, "If Only . . . Detecting the Early Warning Signs for Suicide in Children," The Ohio State University Extension, http://ohioline.osu.edu/flm01/FS09.html.

6. Mayo Foundation for Medical Education and Research, "Suicide: Offering help and support when someone is suicidal," http://www.mayoclinic.com/health/suicide/MH00058.

Chapter 25

7. Based on renting an economy car at $11.97 per day in May 2007 and travel of less than 150 miles per day. Cost includes rental, sales tax, fees, and thirty-four gallons of gas.

8. Based on 2007 figures for St. Louis, MO, and Minneapolis/St. Paul Metro Area.

Chapter 26

9. Based on AAA figures for 2006 for small car, 15,000 miles per year at a cost of 41.4 cents per mile (http://www.aaapublicaffairs.com/Main/Default.asp?CategoryID=3&SubCategoryID=9&ContentID=23).

10. Figures based on generic car wholesale value of 39 percent of purchase price.

Chapter 37

11. United States Department of Health and Human Services, "Surgeon General's Healthy Weight Advice for Consumers," http://www.surgeongeneral.gov/topics/obesity/calltoaction/fact_advice.htm.

12. National Institute of Mental Health, "Depression," http://www.nimh.nih.gov/publicat/depression.cfm#ptdep3.

Chapter 38

13. Based on a person weighing around 150 pounds.

14. Centers for Disease Control and Prevention, "Physical Activity Terms," http://www.cdc.gov/nccdphp/dnpa/physical/terms/index.htm.

15. American Heart Association, "Start! Moving for Individuals," http://www.americanheart.org/presenter.jhtml?identifier=3040779.

Chapter 39

16. The Nemours Foundation, "Hand Washing," http://www.kidshealth.org/teen/your_body/skin_stuff/handwashing.html.

Chapter 40

17. Daniel J. DeNoon, "Drink More Diet Soda, Gain More Weight," FoxNews.com, http://www.foxnews.com/story/0,2933,159579,00.html.

Chapter 44

18. Providence Health System, "Common Medical Costs: The Cost of Care," http://www.providence.org/health_plans/carecosts.htm.

19. Sandra Block, "Oh, to be young and uninsured: Bad idea," *USA Today*, http://www.usatoday.com/money/perfi/credit/2006-12-28-young-debt-insured_x.htm.

Chapter 46

20. The Heimlich Institute, "The Heimlich Maneuver for CHOKING ADULTS," http://www.heimlichinstitute.org/page.php?id=34.

Chapter 51

21. U.S. Department of Health and Human Services, "Are you Web savvy?" http://family.samhsa.gov/monitor/internet.aspx.

Chapter 52

22. National Consumer's League, "2006 Top 10 Internet Scam Trends from NCL's Fraud Center," http://fraud.org/stats/2006/internet.pdf

23. Federal Trade Commission, "Identity Theft Victim Complaint Data," http://www.consumer.gov/idtheft/pdf/clearinghouse_2005.pdf.

24. MSNBC, "Most teens say they've met strangers online," *Dateline NBC*, http://www.msnbc.msn.com/id/12502825/.

25. Clint Van Zandt, "Beware of Cyber Stalkers," *The Abrams Report*, http://www.msnbc.msn.com/id/11101454/.

26. F-Secure Corporation, "F-Secure's Data Security Wrap-Up 2006: January–June," http://www.f-secure.com/2006/1/.

27. Wells Publishing, Inc., "A Computer Hacker Strikes Every 39 Seconds, Warns U. of Md. Study," *Insurance Journal*, http://www.insurancejournal.com/news/national/2007/02/07/76755.htm?print=1.

28. Internet Crime Complaint Center, "Internet Crime Report," http://www.ic3.gov/media/annualreport/2006_IC3Report.pdf.

29. Identity Theft Resource Center, "Facts and Statistics: Find out more about the nation's fastest growing crime," http://www.idtheftmostwanted.org/artman2/publish/m_facts/Facts_and_Statistics.shtml.

30. David Robertson, quoted in "Study: Internet gambling stakes are high" by Thom Patterson, CNN.com, http://archives.cnn.com/2002/HEALTH/conditions/03/17/internet.gambling/index.html.

31. Covenant Eyes, Inc., "Internet Porn," http://www.covenanteyes.com/help_and_support/article/?a=150.

32. The Barna Group, Ltd., "Fewer Than 1 in 10 Teenagers Believe That Music Piracy Is Morally Wrong," http://www.barna.org/FlexPage.aspx?Page=BarnaUpdate&BarnaUpdateID=162.

Chapter 60

33. Selective Service System, "Registration Information," http://www.sss.gov/when.htm.

Chapter 61

34. In most states a felon is permitted to vote after a certain amount of time as passed; but in other states a felon is *never* eligible to vote. Each state has different laws regarding the voting rights of felons. See page 3 of "Felony Disenfranchisement Laws in the United States," www.sentencingproject.org/Admin/Documents/publications/fd_bs_fdlawsinus.pdf.

Index